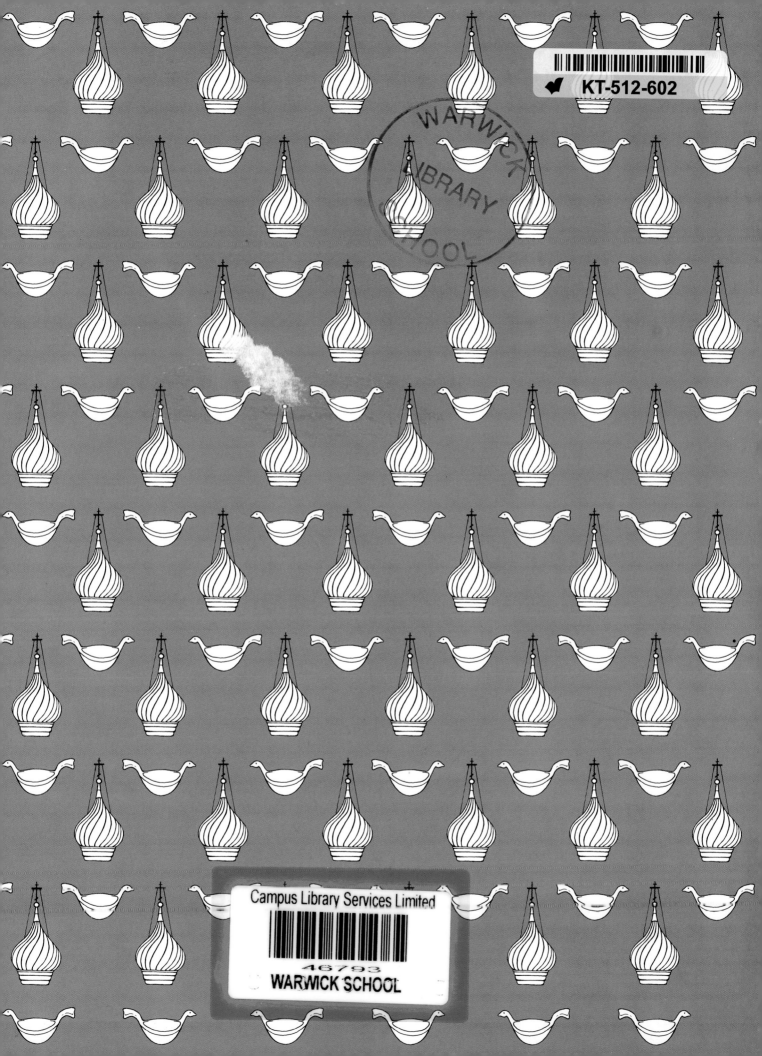

18th-century festive headdress for a married woman

Flag of the Russian Soviet Federal Socialist Republic from 1920 to 1954

Icon of St. Nicholas

Silver *samovar* for making tea

Soviet leader Joseph Stalin

Yury Dolgoruky, founder of Moscow

RUSSIA

Wooden coat of arms
for Russia, 1882

Hat pin of
Cossack leader
Bodgdan
Khmelnitsky

Written by
KATHLEEN BERTON MURRELL

Photographed by
ANDY CRAWFORD

Civil War
sabre owned
by General
Tulenov

Red Army *shlam* hat

Brightly painted
19th-century
cotton spinner

DORLING KINDERSLEY
London • New York
Stuttgart • Moscow • Sydney

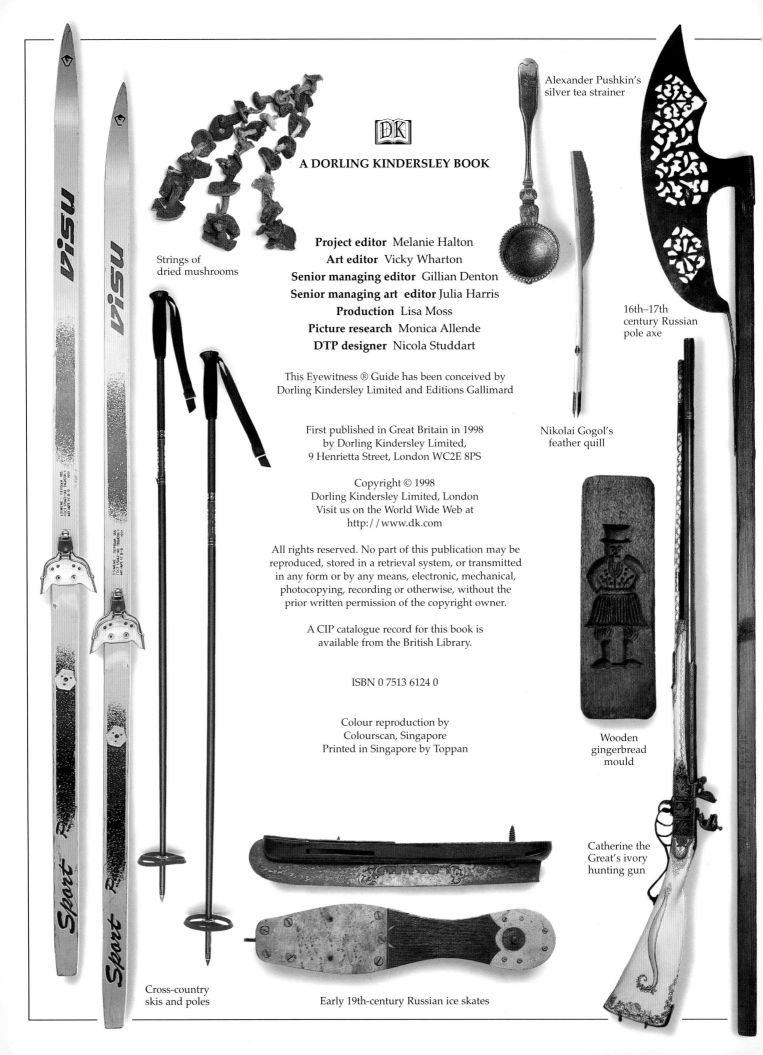

Strings of
dried mushrooms

A DORLING KINDERSLEY BOOK

Project editor Melanie Halton
Art editor Vicky Wharton
Senior managing editor Gillian Denton
Senior managing art editor Julia Harris
Production Lisa Moss
Picture research Monica Allende
DTP designer Nicola Studdart

This Eyewitness ® Guide has been conceived by
Dorling Kindersley Limited and Editions Gallimard

First published in Great Britain in 1998
by Dorling Kindersley Limited,
9 Henrietta Street, London WC2E 8PS

ISBN 0 7513 6124 0

Colour reproduction by
Colourscan, Singapore
Printed in Singapore by Toppan

Alexander Pushkin's
silver tea strainer

16th–17th
century Russian
pole axe

Nikolai Gogol's
feather quill

Wooden
gingerbread
mould

Catherine the
Great's ivory
hunting gun

Cross-country
skis and poles

Early 19th-century Russian ice skates

Contents

Lenin's funeral train

8
Early Russia
10
A varied land
12
Peoples of Russia
14
Wealth of a nation
16
A life of serfdom
18
Orthodox religion
20
Rule of the tsars
22
Empire building
24
Life at court
26
City of domes
28
Palaces of St. Petersburg
30
Bolshevik Revolution
32
The Civil War
34
The rise of Stalin
36
Soviet Russia
38
Rail and industry

40
Science pioneers
42
Media and communications
44
Famous writers
46
Art and icons
48
Music and dance
50
Crafts and traditions
52
Childhood
54
National pastimes
56
Annual festivals
58
The new Russia
60
Index

Early Russia

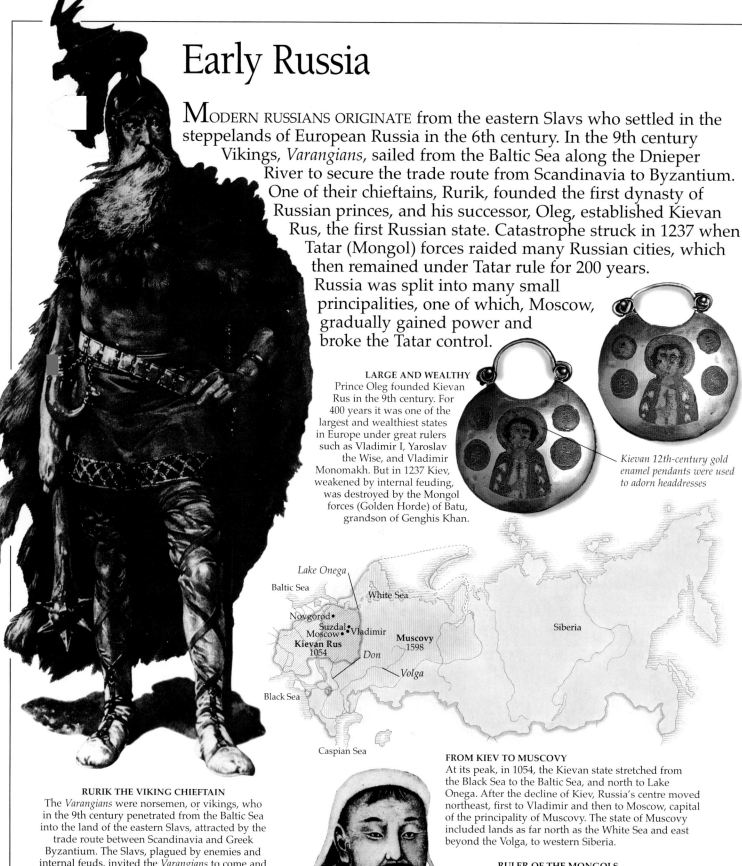

MODERN RUSSIANS ORIGINATE from the eastern Slavs who settled in the steppelands of European Russia in the 6th century. In the 9th century Vikings, *Varangians*, sailed from the Baltic Sea along the Dnieper River to secure the trade route from Scandinavia to Byzantium. One of their chieftains, Rurik, founded the first dynasty of Russian princes, and his successor, Oleg, established Kievan Rus, the first Russian state. Catastrophe struck in 1237 when Tatar (Mongol) forces raided many Russian cities, which then remained under Tatar rule for 200 years. Russia was split into many small principalities, one of which, Moscow, gradually gained power and broke the Tatar control.

LARGE AND WEALTHY
Prince Oleg founded Kievan Rus in the 9th century. For 400 years it was one of the largest and wealthiest states in Europe under great rulers such as Vladimir I, Yaroslav the Wise, and Vladimir Monomakh. But in 1237 Kiev, weakened by internal feuding, was destroyed by the Mongol forces (Golden Horde) of Batu, grandson of Genghis Khan.

Kievan 12th-century gold enamel pendants were used to adorn headdresses

RURIK THE VIKING CHIEFTAIN
The *Varangians* were norsemen, or vikings, who in the 9th century penetrated from the Baltic Sea into the land of the eastern Slavs, attracted by the trade route between Scandinavia and Greek Byzantium. The Slavs, plagued by enemies and internal feuds, invited the *Varangians* to come and rule over them. One of the *Varangian* chieftains, Rurik, took up the challenge to become prince of Novgorod in 862. The few norsemen were soon absorbed by the Slavs and the House of Rurik reigned until the end of the 16th century.

FROM KIEV TO MUSCOVY
At its peak, in 1054, the Kievan state stretched from the Black Sea to the Baltic Sea, and north to Lake Onega. After the decline of Kiev, Russia's centre moved northeast, first to Vladimir and then to Moscow, capital of the principality of Muscovy. The state of Muscovy included lands as far north as the White Sea and east beyond the Volga, to western Siberia.

RULER OF THE MONGOLS
From his base in Asia, the remarkable Mongol leader Genghis Khan conquered China, northern India, what is now Pakistan, and Central Asia. Later, in 1222, he swept into southern Russia with his brilliant mounted troops, plundering the land between the Volga and Dnieper rivers. His grandson, Batu, completed the domination of Russia in 1237, taking most of Kievan Rus and the newer towns of Vladimir and Suzdal before riding west to conquer Hungary and Poland.

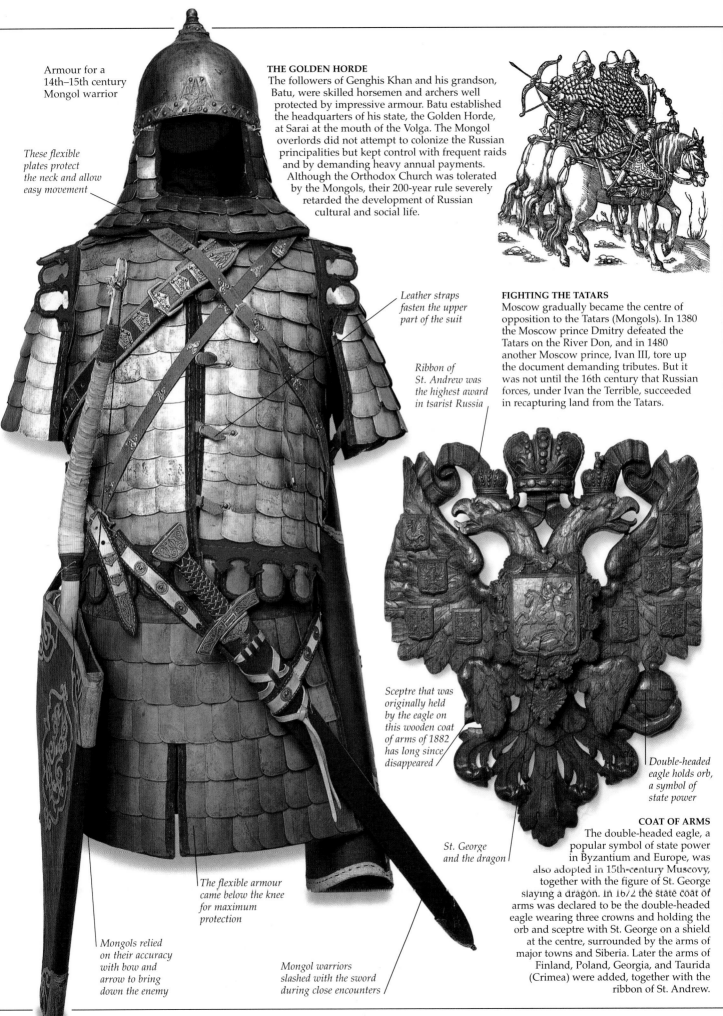

Armour for a
14th–15th century
Mongol warrior

These flexible
plates protect
the neck and allow
easy movement

THE GOLDEN HORDE
The followers of Genghis Khan and his grandson,
Batu, were skilled horsemen and archers well
protected by impressive armour. Batu established
the headquarters of his state, the Golden Horde,
at Sarai at the mouth of the Volga. The Mongol
overlords did not attempt to colonize the Russian
principalities but kept control with frequent raids
and by demanding heavy annual payments.
Although the Orthodox Church was tolerated
by the Mongols, their 200-year rule severely
retarded the development of Russian
cultural and social life.

Leather straps
fasten the upper
part of the suit

Ribbon of
St. Andrew was
the highest award
in tsarist Russia

FIGHTING THE TATARS
Moscow gradually became the centre of
opposition to the Tatars (Mongols). In 1380
the Moscow prince Dmitry defeated the
Tatars on the River Don, and in 1480
another Moscow prince, Ivan III, tore up
the document demanding tributes. But it
was not until the 16th century that Russian
forces, under Ivan the Terrible, succeeded
in recapturing land from the Tatars.

Sceptre that was
originally held
by the eagle on
this wooden coat
of arms of 1882
has long since
disappeared

Double-headed
eagle holds orb,
a symbol of
state power

The flexible armour
came below the knee
for maximum
protection

Mongols relied
on their accuracy
with bow and
arrow to bring
down the enemy

St. George
and the dragon

Mongol warriors
slashed with the sword
during close encounters

COAT OF ARMS
The double-headed eagle, a
popular symbol of state power
in Byzantium and Europe, was
also adopted in 15th-century Muscovy,
together with the figure of St. George
slaying a dragon. In 1672 the state coat of
arms was declared to be the double-headed
eagle wearing three crowns and holding the
orb and sceptre with St. George on a shield
at the centre, surrounded by the arms of
major towns and Siberia. Later the arms of
Finland, Poland, Georgia, and Taurida
(Crimea) were added, together with the
ribbon of St. Andrew.

A varied land

RUSSIA IS THE LARGEST country in the world, straddling the two continents of Europe and Asia and crossing 11 time zones. Its three geographical regions are European Russia in the west, up to the low-lying Ural Mountains; the huge flat expanse of Siberia; and the mountainous far eastern region. The climate is extreme, varying from averages of -20°C (-4°F) in winter to +20°C (68°F) in summer. Russia's mighty rivers include the Volga, Europe's longest river, and the Yenisei in Siberia. Huge Lake Baikal in eastern Siberia is the deepest in the world and contains one-fifth of the world's fresh water. Russia's rich variety of animal life includes tigers, reindeer, moose, sable, polar bears, walrus, and the unique Baikal seal.

Reins attached to these notches are used to steer the sleigh

SOLITARY TIGER
The magnificent Siberian tiger, the largest tiger in the world, lives in solitude in the forests and mountains of the far eastern Ussuri region. Although the number of Siberian tigers fell disastrously to about 20 in the 1940s, a policy of protection has ensured their survival. By the mid-1990s, about 300 were known to exist.

SYMBOL OF A NATION
The common brown bear, one of the national symbols of Russia, lives in the mountains and forests of the entire country from Europe to Siberia, and in the mountains of the far eastern Ussuri region. Such large creatures can sustain themselves in semi-hibernation throughout the winter on the fruits and berries of the forests; on fish; and even on deer, for they can cover short distances at enormous speed.

Traditionally drawn by three horses, a Russian sleigh is often called a troika *from the Russian for "three"*

Curved front shields passengers from spray kicked up by the horses

Animal furs make snug blankets for passengers

IN A COLD CLIMATE
Surprisingly, Russia's severe climate has not impeded winter travel, for roads of packed snow are smoother than the ruts of summer or the muddy tracks of spring and autumn. Horse-drawn sleighs, such as this one, can travel rapidly over snowy highways while passengers recline snugly under the furs. In the past, when sleighs travelled long distances, horses were changed at government post stations, placed at regular intervals along the main routes. Although, on the whole, sleighs have now been replaced by motorized vehicles, they are still used in some rural areas.

Step enables passengers to climb into and out of the sleigh easily

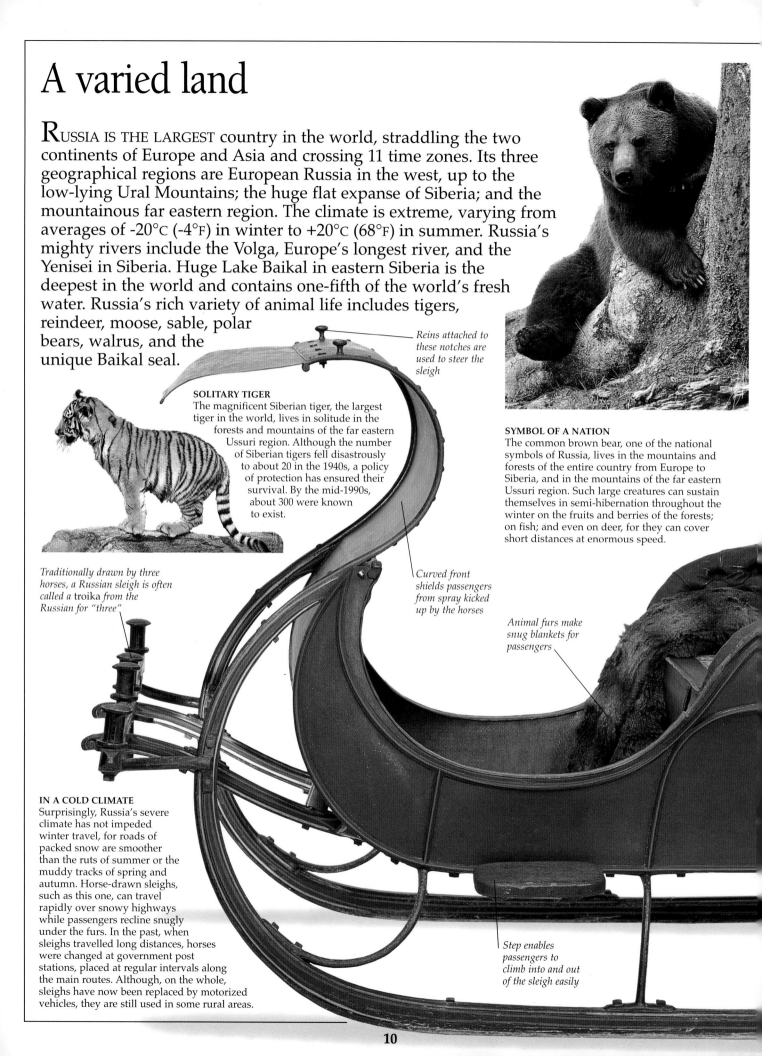

SIBERIAN SURVIVAL
This ivory carving shows how the reindeer makes it possible for people to live in the isolated parts of northern Siberia. Indigenous (native) peoples, such as the Chukchi, rely on domesticated reindeer herds to provide transportation, meat, milk, and hides for clothing and tents.

VEGETATION ZONES
Russia can be divided into broad horizontal bands of vegetation: the treeless tundra in the north, which widens eastwards to include the far eastern region; the taiga, the great forests that dominate most of Russia; and the steppes, or meadowlands, in the south.

TUNDRA SUMMER
In June and July the warm Sun thaws the Arctic soil a few inches down to the permafrost, permanently frozen earth over 1 km (0.62 miles) thick. During this time, the normally bleak landscape is briefly transformed by brightly coloured flowers and green grasses.

In Verkhoyansk, the coldest inhabited place in the world, temperatures can drop to -71°C (-96°F)

Arctic Ocean

Kamchatka Peninsula

Moscow

Don

Ural Mountains

Volga

Yenisei

Ob

Lena

Siberia

Russian Federation

Lake Baikal

Vladivostok

☐ Steppe
☐ Taiga
☐ Tundra

TAIGA FORESTS
The great taiga forests of larch, pine, spruce, birch, and aspen account for over half of the world's resources of softwood and provide havens for the wide variety of animals that inhabit Russia.

Cushioned backrest provides comfort on long journeys

Handle is gripped by the coachman when the sleigh is in motion

GRASSY PLAINS
Steppes, or treeless grasslands, are distinguished by a thick layer of extremely fertile black earth that is ideal for agriculture. The steppes are found in the southern parts of European Russia and Siberia.

Coachman sits on leather stool during journey

FRIEND OR FOE?
The villain of Russian fairy tales, the large grey wolf is now found only in the wilds of Siberia and the remoter areas of European Russia. With its thick fur, which whitens the further north it travels, it adapts admirably to life in a cold climate. Its poor reputation is undeserved, for although it will kill sheep and farm animals when in desperate hunger, attacks on human beings are very rare.

Coat of arms indicates that this sleigh belonged to an important family

These shoe-shaped leather footrests protect the coachman's feet from the harsh elements

Distinctive black-and-white wing markings

RED-BREASTED GOOSE
Black, white, and chestnut-red, these most vivid of all geese breed in the far northern reaches of Siberia, bordering on the Arctic Ocean. These beautiful birds provide living proof that the huge, almost uninhabited regions of Russia's cold north can support a colourful variety of life during the warmer months of the year, June to August. But the number of breeding pairs has declined by over two-thirds in the past century, mostly because of indiscriminate hunting.

Metal blades stabilize the sleigh as it glides over ice

Peoples of Russia

Before the 1917 Revolution, Russia was a truly multinational empire, which included Ukrainians and Belorussians; Kazakhs and other peoples of Central Asia; Georgians, Armenians, and Azerbaijanis in the Caucasus region; Lithuanians, Latvians, and Estonians in the north; Tatars; Germans; and many others. Even present-day Russia, with its reduced borders, has over 100 nationalities. But whereas Russians before the break-up of the Soviet Union accounted for just over one-half of the total population, and were a minority in the Russian empire, they now form 82 per cent of the 150 million people of the new Russian State.

Soft swan down pompom

COSSACKS
Russians largely made up the Cossack (p. 23) self-governing communities in the Kuban, Astrakhan, and Orenburg provinces in the south. However, some Cossack settlements were not Russian but Kalmyk and Buryat (Mongol peoples), Bashkir (Turkic-speaking), and Tungus (native Siberian).

KOKOSHNIK
Red velvet hats, like this one, were Russian women's everyday wear for centuries. All but the highest nobility wore the *kokoshnik*.

FAMILY HEIRLOOM
This festive 19th-century outfit with its delightful pompom hat comes from the Ryazan area, south of Moscow. The owner would have made the blouse, skirt, apron, and sleeveless jacket herself. She would have spun the linen thread from flax, then woven the material, and sewn the clothes together. Finally she would have done all the embroidery and crochet work. Such a fine outfit would have been handed down within the family.

Ryazan designs are typically geometric

Apron displays fine crochet work

NATIONAL DRESS
A sleeveless dress, *sarafan,* and *kokoshnik* hat were the accepted costume for Russian peasant and servant women all over the country until the 20th century. The decoration and colour of the *sarafan* differed greatly from district to district.

REPUBLIC OF TATARSTAN
Turkic-speaking Tatars form about 4 per cent of the population of Russia – about 6 million people. Most live in the Republic of Tatarstan within the Russian Federation. They are descendants of the Golden Horde (p. 11) and many of them are Muslims. In 1994 Tatarstan signed a treaty giving it special rights within the Federation.

Hooded costume of Tatar women reflects the now rare custom of veil wearing

Hood prevents loss of body heat and keeps head and ears warm in sub-zero temperatures

Tungus nomad

Tungus town dweller

Men of Tobolsk

NATIVES OF SIBERIA
Today Russians greatly outnumber the many small groups of indigenous (native) Siberian peoples. The two native Siberians (above right) are from the Tobolsk area west of the Urals. Those on the left are Tungus from the Amur district on the border of China. The one in the long fur-lined coat is a town dweller and next to him is a nomad, who lives with his reindeer herds.

Mittens are sewn into the sleeves to keep out biting winds

THE NORTHERN PEOPLE
This warm coat belongs to the Nganasan people, the most northerly inhabitants of Russia, whose way of life resembles that of the Inuit. They are one of the least numerous peoples of the Samoyed-Nenets group, and live on the Taimyr Peninsula in northern Siberia. They lived traditionally as nomadic hunters, reindeer herders, and fishermen, although in the Soviet period many were forced to settle on collective farms.

Wealth of a nation

RUSSIA HAS VAST reserves of natural resources, from timber – about one-fifth of all the world's forests – to a remarkable supply of rocks and minerals. These include huge deposits of gold, diamonds, iron ore, copper, nickel, lead, and zinc. There are also large deposits of fossil fuels including coal – half the world's reserves – oil, peat, and natural gas. Fur trapping, Russia's earliest source of wealth, is still practised. Fishing, particularly for sturgeon, is a highly developed industry, and Russia's long rivers are used to generate over 10 per cent of the world's hydroelectric power.

Polished amber bead

Crystallized gold nugget

DIAMOND DISCOVERY
Until the 19th century diamonds, such as those in the imperial crown (above) were imported from India. Russian diamonds were first discovered in 1955 in an isolated spot in north central Siberia. Within a year a new town, Mirny, had been built. It has good links by air but the nearest railroad is over 1,000 km (621 miles) away. However, Mirny is now a town of about 40,000 people, who are mostly involved in diamond production.

ANCIENT AMBER
Light gold to dark brown, amber is an ancient fossilized resin that has long been valued. Since at least 2,000 BCE it has been gathered along the Baltic shores of Russia and used for trade in the Mediterranean. Catherine Palace (p. 29) was famous for its room lined with panels of amber.

MINING FOR MINERALS
Iron ore and other metals are especially abundant in Siberia. The northern Siberian town of Norilsk (p. 39), beyond the Arctic Circle, was founded in the 1930s to extract rich deposits of nickel, copper, and cobalt, and now also produces gold, silver, and platinum.

GOLD RUSH
Russia has some of the largest gold reserves in the world. In 1838 a discovery near the Yenisei River in Siberia, followed by huge finds near the upper Lena River, started a gold rush. In 1923 another major find was made at Aldan on the upper Lena.

Russian nobleman in fur-lined coat and fur hat

Furry side flaps untie to cover ears in particularly cold weather

Front flap folds down to cover forehead

FUR TRAPPING
To combat the harsh cold of winter, most Russians wear fur hats and coats with the fur on the inside. Animals are still trapped extensively in the wild, mostly by native peoples. There are also many fur farms where mink, sable, and fox are raised for their skins. But the fur of animals living in the wild is considered the best.

FUR TRADERS
Early traders from central Russia were lured north and east in search of the pelts of animals from the Russian Arctic. By the 17th century fur was the most important item of foreign trade for the merchants of Moscow. The annual fur auction in St. Petersburg is still considered the most important fur market in the world.

Deep green with pale green streaks, malachite is a popular stone for carving into objects, such as this 19th-century vase from Yekaterinburg in the Urals

NATURAL GAS
The leading producer of fossil fuels, Russia has 40 per cent of the world's natural gas. Deposits lie in the northern Caucasus, Siberia, and along the Arctic coast. Pipelines laid in the 1970s and 1980s, linking the Siberian gas fields with European Russia greatly eased transportation difficulties. Huge gas exports help to pay for Russian imports.

Laying pipelines in northern Russia is difficult and costly because of permafrost (p. 11)

MIGHTY STURGEON
As the Volga and the Caspian Sea become polluted, the huge sturgeon that provide caviar (fish eggs) – a popular Russian dish and much sought after export – are becoming scarce. Nevertheless, with a large modern fleet, fishing is a major industry in Russia, not only along the seas that border its coasts, but also further afield in the Atlantic and Pacific.

MALACHITE
This beautiful green copper compound occurs in only four places in the world, including the Ural Mountains of Russia. In the 19th century, malachite was used to make jewellery, furniture, and beautiful objects, such as this vase, for high society. The interior walls of the Malachite Hall in the Winter Palace (p. 20), a room for ceremonial occasions, are completely lined with the bright green stone.

Arms move up and down as if washing the bear in the tub

Traditional Russian toy carved from wood

HYDROELECTRICITY
With its vast water resources, Russia has built many dams to generate electricity. Stalin favoured huge hydroelectric projects, such as reversing the flow of rivers, but recently these have been rejected because they would damage the environment.

TIMBER
Russia has about one-fifth of the world's forests and nearly half the world's softwood (pine and other conifers). Siberian forests are remote, so tree felling is concentrated nearer to markets in central Russia and the Urals. The wood is used to make paper, furniture, and village houses, and much is still used as firewood.

A life of serfdom

THE ARISTOCRATS
Until the end of the 17th century, tsars and the aristocracy shared the same culture, language, and religion as the peasants. But as Peter the Great (pp. 20, 22) forced the nobles to shave their beards and adopt Western dress, customs, and languages, the gap between aristocrats and peasants widened immensely.

SERFS WERE PEASANTS bound to their landlord's estates and forced to work the land. They were virtually slaves, for they could do nothing without their lord's approval – not even marry. They could be bought and sold, exiled to Siberia, or forced to join the army. But the law forbade landlords to kill their serfs. Until the 17th century, on one day each year, serfs were allowed to move to another estate. In 1649, even this freedom was abolished. Two centuries later, in 1861, serfs were finally freed. The liberated serfs provided labour for new industry, leading to spectacular economic growth. But peasants had to pay heavily for the land they believed was theirs by right; freedom brought little improvement to their lives.

ESSENTIAL TOOLS
Peasants on Russia's large estates continued to use wooden agricultural implements, scarcely improved since medieval times, until well into the 20th century. Most landlords, with unlimited cheap peasant labour, did little to improve the land or farming methods. But some, such as the writer Tolstoy, supported more progressive farming techniques.

LOG HOUSES
Villages with identical log houses, called *izbas*, are still common all over Russia, although straw roofs are now rare. The *izba* has one large room for the extended family, dominated by a great stove which is also used as a warm sleeping bench during the long winters.

CAPTURE OF PUGACHEV
Runaway serfs fled to the borderlands in the south and became Cossacks, or free warriors, farming and organizing their communities far from the heavy hand of the tsar. In 1773 Yemelyan Pugachev, a Cossack leader, declared himself Emperor Peter III, murdered husband of Catherine the Great. Promising liberation of the serfs, he led a popular revolt of peasants of Russian and other nationalities in the Volga and Ural regions. He was successful at first, capturing Kazan and threatening Moscow, but was captured at the end of 1774, brought to Moscow in this specially built cage, and publicly tortured and executed.

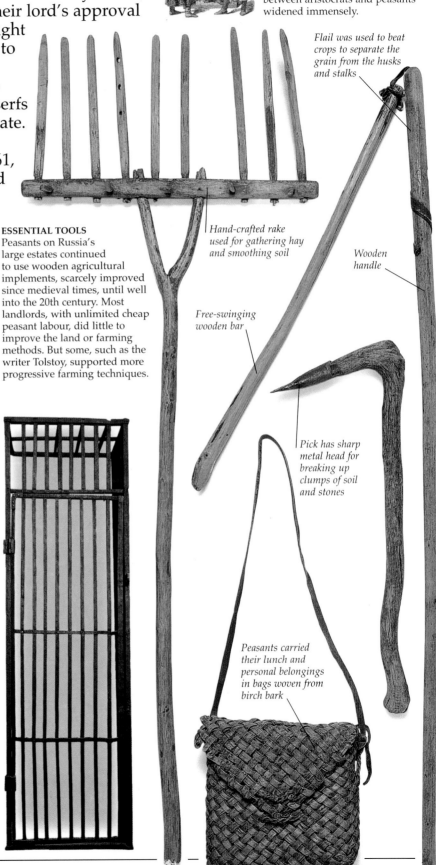

Flail was used to beat crops to separate the grain from the husks and stalks

Hand-crafted rake used for gathering hay and smoothing soil

Wooden handle

Free-swinging wooden bar

Pick has sharp metal head for breaking up clumps of soil and stones

Peasants carried their lunch and personal belongings in bags woven from birch bark

*Loose linen blouse
with lace-up collar
kept peasants cool
on hot summer days*

PEASANT LIFE

Before the Revolution of 1917,
four out of five persons in
Russia were peasants. Only
one-fifth were literate, but
they were skilful craftsmen
able to construct their own
houses, spin cloth, and make
all their own agricultural
tools. Peasants belonged to a
tight-knit village commune, or
mir, whose elders were
responsible for collecting
taxes, settling disputes, and
allocating land.

*Brightly coloured
woollen skirts
were homespun*

*Curved blade of the
sickle is used to cut
grass and crops,
such as wheat*

*Female serfs often
wore many layers of
skirts to keep them
warm in the winter*

FREEDOM TO THE PEOPLE

In March 1861, serfs celebrated throughout Russia as
news spread of Tsar Alexander II's emancipation law.
About 50 million Russian people were thus freed from
near slavery. However, the former serfs were still
bound to their communes and in debt for what little
land they received. Many felt cheated and remained
dissatisfied with their situation.

*Traditional serfs' shoes
were hand-woven
from birch bark*

TRADITIONAL ATTIRE

Women's everyday wear was a simple
blouse and skirt, or a sleeveless dress
(*sarafan*). Men wore trousers, linen
shirts, and a caftan. In summer
peasants wore birch-bark shoes (*lapti*),
but in winter they put on felt boots
(*valenki*) which were surprisingly
warm against the snow. Sheepskin
overcoats, the fur turned inwards,
provided warmth in winter. More
elaborate costumes were kept for
special occasions and handed down
from generation to generation.

Orthodox religion

A<small>LTHOUGH MANY RELIGIONS</small>, including Buddhism and Islam, are found in Russia, most of the population identifies with Orthodox Christianity. Adopted from Byzantium over 1,000 years ago by Prince Vladimir, it was chosen for the splendour of its ceremonies. Rich in ritual, Orthodox services are often long, elaborate, and colourful. Priests chant and the choir sings without the accompaniment of musical instruments, because it is believed that only the human voice should be used in sacred music. Orthodoxy remained Russia's State religion until the Revolution in 1917. In the Soviet era many churches were destroyed and priests shot or imprisoned. Since 1992, when official support was renewed, the Church has rapidly revived.

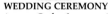

WEDDING CEREMONY
During an Orthodox marriage service, ornate crowns, like the poet Pushkin's (above) are held over the heads of the bride and groom. The couple drink wine three times from the same cup. The priest then leads the couple three times around the centre of the church.

Slanted bar on Russian Orthodox cross represents where Christ's feet were nailed

St. Nicholas, the 4th-century Byzantine bishop

Embossed metal covers this icon, revealing only the hand and face of the painted saint

NIKON'S REFORMS
Patriarch Nikon was head of the Church from 1652 to 1658. His reforms to rituals, such as making the sign of the cross with three fingers instead of two, met with strenuous opposition from a group called the Old Believers, who separated from the Church. When Nikon tried to make the Church more powerful than the State, the tsar imprisoned him in a remote monastery.

SACRED PICTURES
Sculptures were discouraged by the Church for a long time because it was thought that they might become objects of worship. But icons – religious pictures painted on wooden panels – could be venerated (deeply respected) because they are not lifelike images. Icons are found not only in churches, but also in Russian homes.

MONASTERIES
Although most of the ancient monasteries were forced to close after the Bolshevik Revolution and were neglected or destroyed, many have been vigorously revived in the new Russia. The most important is the beautiful Trinity Lavra of St. Sergius, founded in the 14th century. In 1689, the monastery's enterprising monks supported Peter the Great in his struggle for the throne against his half-sister, Sophia.

Oil lamp for lighting up icons

Apostle Matthew

Apostle John

Angel tells Mary she will bear the son of God

Apostle Luke

Apostle Mark

ROYAL DOORS
The royal doors are at the centre of the iconostasis – the tall wall of tiered, religious paintings that screens the altar from the rest of the church. The congregation stands throughout the service, facing the iconostasis. Only the clergy are permitted to enter through the royal doors which are opened at certain moments during services, symbolically revealing heaven to the faithful.

CHURCH CLERGY
At the head of the Church is the patriarch. He, like all senior ranks of the Orthodox Church – the metropolitans, archbishops, bishops, and archimandrites – is drawn from the unmarried "black" clergy (monks). The more numerous priests, the "white" clergy, are normally married and often remain parish priests all their lives. Women are not permitted to enter the clergy.

Orthodox bishop

Golden chalice

Mitre symbolizes a bishop's power

Bishop's mitre

Elaborately bound Book of the Gospels

HOLY BOOK
The Bible was translated into Old Church Slavonic in the 9th century by Saints Cyril and Methodius. Church Slavonic is close to the Russian language and is still used today in church services.

Stole, omoforion, is worn only by bishops

Palitza, *which hangs from the right hip, is worn by bishops and some senior priests*

Sacchos *hangs down to the mid-calf*

Girdle

Cuffs are laced around the wrist

Sacchos, or bishop's vestment, symbolizes the robe of Christ

CEREMONIAL ROBES
The robes for ceremonial occasions in the Orthodox Church are often magnificent and richly coloured, as these bishop's vestments portray. Each item of clothing has a special religious significance. Both bishops and priests normally wear a black cassock, or robe, and a black hat (*skufya*). For services, priests have their own special vestments, many of which are similar to those of the bishop. More ornate robes are worn by bishops and priests for Easter and other important festivals.

Staff, or crosier, signifies that the bishop is a shepherd of his people

Priestly stole, epitrachelion, hangs down almost to the floor

Rule of the tsars

R USSIA HAS KNOWN two royal dynasties; the Rurikids (c. 860–1598) and, following the Time of Troubles (c. 1605–13), the Romanovs (1613–1917). The chaotic Time of Troubles was a period of civil strife when many pretenders fought for the throne, and unrest, famine, and invasion plagued the country. Russian princes adopted the title "tsar" from the Roman "Caesar" in the 15th century, as the power and prestige of Moscow grew. The title "emperor" came into use in the 18th century under Peter the Great. Tsars throughout Russian history ruled with absolute power.

THE ROMANOV DYNASTY
In 1613, 16-year-old Mikhail Romanov was elected to the throne. His family continued to rule for the next 300 years. The dynasty ended in February 1917 when Nicholas II abdicated (gave up the throne).

Gold crown studded with pearls, garnets, and turquoise

Sable-fur trimming made crown more comfortable to wear

CROWN OF KAZAN
Thought to have belonged to Ediger Mahmet, this 16th-century crown is one of the oldest in Russia. Mahmet was the last ruler of the Tatar state of Kazan. He adopted Christianity and became loyal to Ivan the Terrible.

IVAN THE TERRIBLE
Ivan IV's long rule (1533–84) began hopefully, with new laws, territorial conquests, and commercial relations with England. After the death of his first wife, however, Ivan began a reign of terror, even murdering his own son.

Peter and Paul Fortress in St. Petersburg, painted 1723

Porcelain frame decorated with enamel on copper

BORIS GODUNOV
Unpopular Boris Godunov ruled at the end of the Rurikid dynasty. He was suspected of murdering the rightful heir, Prince Dmitry. Godunov died suddenly in 1605, resulting in a prolonged battle for a successor – the Time of Troubles had begun.

PETER THE GREAT
Peter I, who took the throne by force from his half-sister, Sophia, ruled from 1689 to 1725. The most energetic of the tsars, he founded a new capital city (pp. 28–29), established the navy (p. 22), initiated radical reforms in education and government, and was the first tsar to travel abroad.

CATHERINE II
Born a German princess, Catherine became Empress of Russia in 1762, and ruled for over 30 years. Known as Catherine the Great, she was the last of four strong empresses to rule after Peter I.

DECEMBRIST REVOLT
Throughout Russian history, there were many peasant uprisings against tsarist rule. But the 1825 revolt against Nicholas I by the aristocratic Decembrists shocked the regime. With little support, the revolt soon died out. Five of the leaders were hanged and the rest condemned to hard labour in Siberia.

Executed leaders of the Decembrist Revolt

Ring made from chains that bound Decembrists in Siberia

Cupid holds the orb and sceptre, which are symbols of state power

Empress Elizabeth's monogram

Imperial coat of arms – St. George and the double-headed eagle

Golden embroidery on red velvet

Carved and gilded female head

TSARS' SECRET POLICE
The notorious secret police of the tsars, the Third Department (later the Okhrana) infiltrated and suppressed revolutionary organizations. But the organization's cruelty pales beside the brutality of the Soviet secret police, the NKVD (later the KGB).

Like all Russian tsars, Alexander II was an accomplished horseman

ALEXANDER II
The highlight of Alexander's reign was the emancipation of the serfs in 1861. But the reforming tsar was killed by a terrorist's bomb in 1881. His successor, Alexander III, pursued harsh, reactionary policies, reversing many of his father's reforms.

Nicholas and Alexandra wear 17th-century tsarist costumes for a grand ball, 1903

STRONG EMPRESSES, WEAK EMPERORS
After the death of Peter I in 1725, the rest of the 18th century was dominated by strong empresses, such as Peter I's daughter, Elizabeth, and German-born Catherine II. Assisted by elite guards, each took the throne by force from weak emperors, and both enjoyed the popularity of the general public. The ornate decoration of Elizabeth's gilded throne (above) is typical of her extravagant taste. Both Elizabeth and Catherine were responsible for most of the opulent palaces and royal estates in and around St. Petersburg.

LAST IN LINE
Nicholas II celebrated the tercentenary of the Romanov dynasty in 1913. Four years later, however, following the catastrophe of war and civil rioting, he abdicated on behalf of himself and his haemophilic son. The tsar and his family were murdered by the Bolsheviks in 1918 (p. 32).

Empire building

THE HISTORY OF Russia is one of almost continual expansion. It has been estimated that from 1600 to 1900 Russia grew at a rate of 130 square km (50 square miles) a day! With no natural barriers to the east or west, Russia lay open to repeated invasions throughout its history. After gaining strength, Russia expanded its frontiers, partly to protect its vulnerable heartland. By the end of the 18th century, Russia included Siberia, western Ukraine, Lithuania, Poland, and Tatar Crimea. In 1809, Finland was added, and in the first half of the 19th century, the small countries of the Caucasus – Georgia, Armenia, and Azerbaijan – and huge areas of Central Asia became part of the empire.

FOUNDER OF THE RUSSIAN FLEET
Peter the Great, the first tsar to interest himself in naval matters, founded the Russian fleet after studying shipbuilding in Holland and England. In the Great Northern War with Sweden (1700–21) he expanded Russian territory to the Baltic Sea, gaining Swedish territory in southern Finland, the marshes on which he built his new capital, St. Petersburg, and what are now Estonia and Latvia. Peter the Great also captured the long peninsula of Kamchatka and the Kurile Islands in the Pacific Ocean.

Hatpin of Ukrainian Cossack leader Bogdan Khmelnitsky

Brass gun barrel

Porcelain cup showing General Bagration

Type of cannon employed at the Battle of Borodino

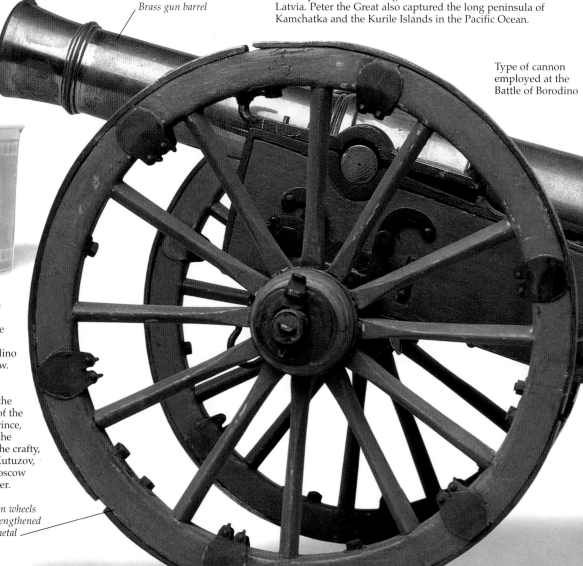

BAGRATION AT BORODINO
Napoleon, at the head of the half-million strong French army, invaded Russia in June 1812. By September, he had succeeded in reaching Borodino on the approaches to Moscow. A bloody battle broke out in which many were mortally wounded, including one of the most brilliant commanders of the Russian army, a Georgian prince, Pyotr Bagration. Following the battle, the Russians, led by the crafty, one-eyed Marshal Mikhail Kutuzov, retreated. Napoleon took Moscow but was driven out in October.

Wooden wheels are strengthened with metal

IMPERIAL EMPIRE

By 1914 the Russian empire was by far the largest in the world, stretching from the Arctic Ocean to the Caspian Sea and from the Baltic Sea to the Pacific. Within its borders were diverse nationalities ranging from the northern ice-bound Chukchi to the desert nomads of Kazakhstan. The huge empire, which included Finland and Poland, was divided into provinces and ruled from St. Petersburg.

Defence of Sevastopol 1854–55

CRIMEAN WAR

In the Crimean War (1853–56), Russia fought against Britain, France, and Turkey. Russia, badly led and poorly supplied, was defeated despite the heroic year-long defence of Sevastopol, on the Black Sea, and a naval victory against Turkey. Under the peace treaty, Russia kept the Crimea, but its power in the Black Sea was weakened.

EXPLORING ALASKA

Fur-rich Alaska, separated from Siberia by narrow straits, was first visited by Russians in 1741. In 1789 Joseph Billings, an English sailor in Russian service, led a secret expedition to study Alaska's peoples and explore its coast. The United States bought Alaska in 1867.

Letter of July 1791 carved on walrus tusk, and sent to Billings from Siberia, documents landings on Alaskan coast

RUNAWAY SERFS

The first Cossacks were runaway serfs who formed frontier settlements in southern Russia and Ukraine. At first, Cossacks opposed the Russian authorities, but by the 19th century they had turned their settlements into prosperous agricultural communities and were fiercely loyal to the tsar.

Cossack shashka sword

CONQUEST OF SIBERIA

Ivan the Terrible opened the way to the resources of Siberia when he defeated the Tatars at Kazan on the Volga. Yermak, a daring Cossack leader, penetrated further into fur-rich western Siberia in 1581, as shown in Surikov's painting of 1895. With 840 men he conquered the native tribes and greatly expanded Russia's borders.

Cannons were dragged to their battle positions by horses

MILITARY COSSACKS

Cossacks wore distinctive uniforms, with tall fur hats and sheepskin cloaks; they carried a sword like this *shashka* (right) and a long lance. All Cossack men had to serve in Cossack military units, which were famous for their loyalty, bravery, and fine horsemanship.

DEFEAT OF NAPOLEON

In 1812, the French took Moscow. But a terrible fire destroyed most of the city, including winter supplies. After only one month Napoleon, the conqueror of Europe and Egypt, was forced to retreat. Frozen and starving, 90 per cent of his men died or deserted. Two years later, the Russians, under Alexander I, rode triumphantly into Paris and Russia began to play a prominent role in European affairs.

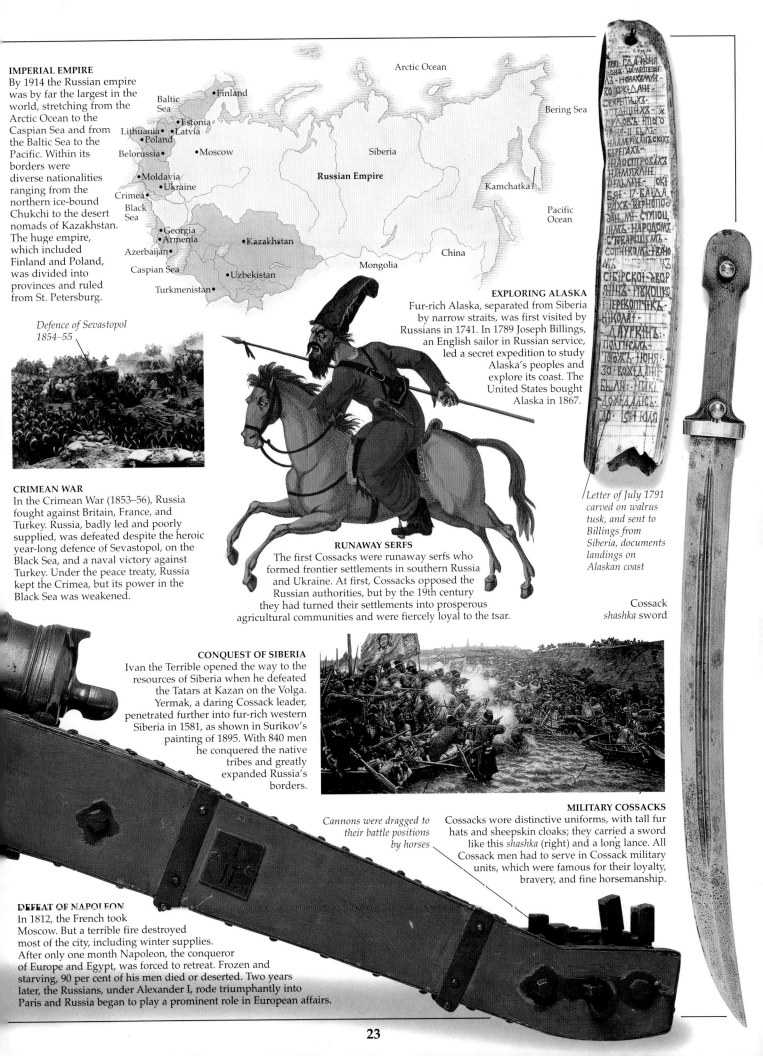

Life at court

Sceptre is decorated with the Orlov diamond, one of the largest in the world

IN MUSCOVITE TIMES (pp. 8–9) the royal court was at the Kremlin in Moscow. Tsars were attended by bearded nobles (_boyars_), wearing ornate costumes. Elaborate court rituals were based on Byzantine customs and those of the former Mongol overlords, such as the deep kowtow (bow). The imperial court at St. Petersburg (1712–1917) adopted Western dress and manners, imitating French King Louis XIV's opulent court of Versailles. The Russian emperor or empress was attended by French-speaking aristocrats.

SILVER SPECTACLES
Catherine the Great was a prolific reader, correspondent, and writer of plays. She used these elegant spectacles, with their enamel case, when working at her desk.

CROWN JEWELS
The diamond-studded Grand Imperial Crown of 1762, made for Catherine II's enthronement, was used in all subsequent coronations. The central band of diamond oak leaves and acorns, symbols of State power, begins with Empress Elizabeth's perfect diamond of 56 carats and ends with a magnificent Chinese ruby of nearly 400 carats.

Gilt cupids adorn the front of the carriage

CORONATION CEREMONY
The crowning of Nicholas II in 1896 (shown above) took place at the Assumption Cathedral, Moscow. Coronations continued to be held in the cathedral after the capital moved to St. Petersburg. Nicholas II's coronation celebrations were horribly marred when 1,200 peasants were killed in a stampede of people waiting to receive royal gifts.

GRAND PALACE BALLS
From the elegant dances held by Alexander I to the sumptuous fancy-dress affairs of the fun-loving Elizabeth, lavish balls were the highlight of the winter season in St. Petersburg. Olga, Nicholas II's eldest daughter, made her debut in 1913 at the last glittering ball held before the Bolshevik Revolution.

Wheels are wooden with metal rims

Two or three pairs of matched horses would have drawn the carriage

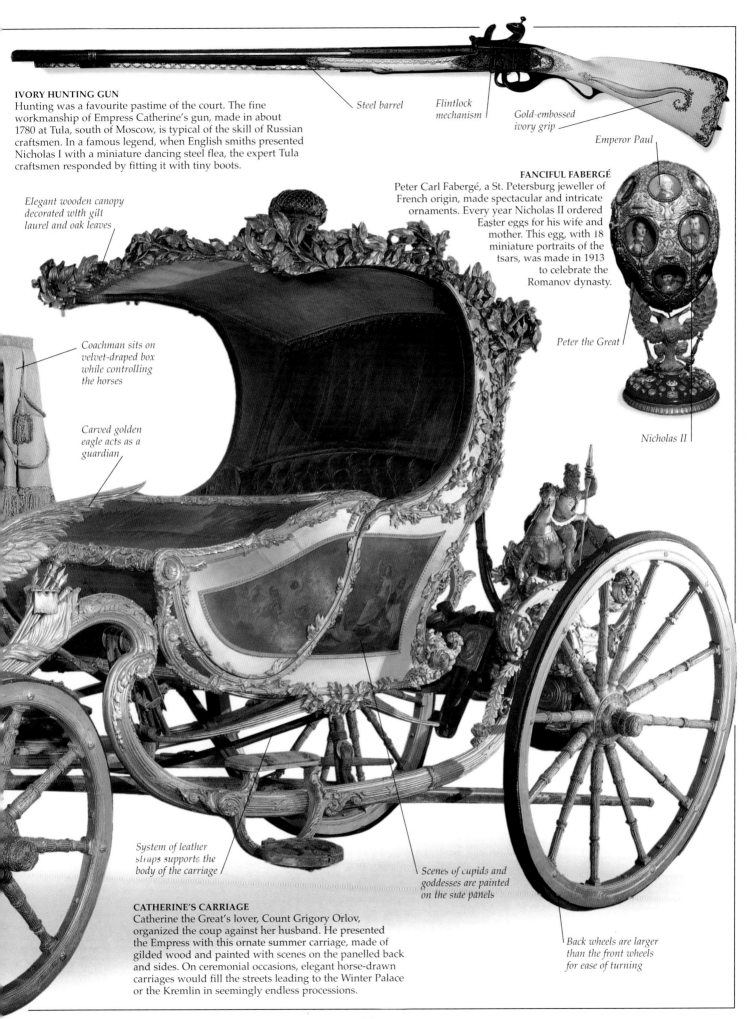

IVORY HUNTING GUN
Hunting was a favourite pastime of the court. The fine workmanship of Empress Catherine's gun, made in about 1780 at Tula, south of Moscow, is typical of the skill of Russian craftsmen. In a famous legend, when English smiths presented Nicholas I with a miniature dancing steel flea, the expert Tula craftsmen responded by fitting it with tiny boots.

Steel barrel

Flintlock mechanism

Gold-embossed ivory grip

Emperor Paul

FANCIFUL FABERGÉ
Peter Carl Fabergé, a St. Petersburg jeweller of French origin, made spectacular and intricate ornaments. Every year Nicholas II ordered Easter eggs for his wife and mother. This egg, with 18 miniature portraits of the tsars, was made in 1913 to celebrate the Romanov dynasty.

Peter the Great

Nicholas II

Elegant wooden canopy decorated with gilt laurel and oak leaves

Coachman sits on velvet-draped box while controlling the horses

Carved golden eagle acts as a guardian

System of leather straps supports the body of the carriage

Scenes of cupids and goddesses are painted on the side panels

CATHERINE'S CARRIAGE
Catherine the Great's lover, Count Grigory Orlov, organized the coup against her husband. He presented the Empress with this ornate summer carriage, made of gilded wood and painted with scenes on the panelled back and sides. On ceremonial occasions, elegant horse-drawn carriages would fill the streets leading to the Winter Palace or the Kremlin in seemingly endless processions.

Back wheels are larger than the front wheels for ease of turning

City of domes

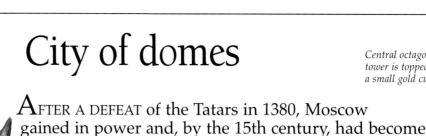

Central octagonal tower is topped by a small gold cupola

AFTER A DEFEAT of the Tatars in 1380, Moscow gained in power and, by the 15th century, had become the leading city of Russia. Although Peter the Great moved the capital to St. Petersburg in 1712, Moscow, the "second capital", still played a major role. In 1812 Napoleon captured Moscow. But the city was soon ablaze – probably set on fire deliberately by its citizens, who preferred to flee rather than surrender. Napoleon's starving army, faced with the onset of winter, was then forced to retreat. The rebuilt city prospered and became capital again in 1918, under the Bolsheviks. Before the October Revolution, Moscow was known for its amazing domed churches but half were destroyed during the Soviet era. In the new Russia, many are being rebuilt.

CITY FOUNDER
Moscow was founded by Prince Yury Dolgoruky. It is first mentioned in early Russian chronicles in 1147, when Dolgoruky invited other princes to a feast. The first wooden fortress was built in 1156, on the hill where the Kremlin now stands.

Kremlin   W   *Red Square*

S   N

E

CITY BOUNDARIES
This 1605 map shows how Moscow developed in a circular pattern. Expanding eastwards from the Kremlin to embrace Red Square, the city then widened in a walled horseshoe around the original core. Wooden palisades (fences) and earthen ramparts (embankments) were built in 1592 to circle the whole wooden town. This old town centre now makes up only 2 per cent of the modern city.

ST. BASIL'S CATHEDRAL
Dominating Red Square is the fantastic Cathedral of the Intercession, better known as St. Basil's. It is named after a holy man who dared to stand up to Ivan the Terrible. The cathedral was built between 1555 and 1561 to celebrate Ivan's victory over the Tatars. It consists of eight chapels topped by ornate cupolas (domes) grouped around the central church tower. Ivan allegedly blinded the architect to ensure this masterpiece could never be rivalled.

All Saints Gate guarding the bridge across the Moscow River

Medieval palaces, including the tsars' Terem Palace

Ivan Veliky bell tower, for many years the tallest building in Moscow

All Saints, or Great Stone Bridge, built in 1692

VIEW OF THE KREMLIN
The Kremlin, the high-walled triangular fortress on the Moscow River, shines with 33 golden domes and contains the great cathedrals and former palaces of the tsars. Italian Renaissance architects built the walls and most of the churches between 1475 and 1505. After the 1917 Revolution, Lenin, and then Stalin, lived and worked in the Kremlin. Today it houses the office of the Russian president.

Onion domes

Cupolas, or domes, first appeared in the north of Russia. The familiar onion shape may have developed because it sheds snow more easily than the shallow Byzantine dome from which it was adapted.

An early helmet-shaped dome

Church of the Intercession, Rubtsovo, 1626

Highly decorated gables

Church of St. Nicholas, Bersenevka, 1657

INTO THE DOME
Pine wood, readily available in northern Russia, was easily shaped by skilful axe men to make the dome. Supported by the king post and spindle beams, three-piece struts were slotted together; nails were not used. The framework was then linked with cross boarding to mould the frame. Wedged outer shingles were of moist aspen which gives a silvery glow.

King post would have supported a tall wooden cross

Scarf joint bonds the two king posts for maximum strength

KIZHI ISLAND CHURCH
The ultimate in northern wooden architecture is the Church of the Transfiguration, built in 1714. Its 22 cupolas rise in elaborate tiers to form a striking silhouette. In the flat landscape these cupolas resemble the pine trees of the surrounding forests.

Wedges ensure sufficient tension

Spindle beams, like spokes in a wheel, provide horizontal support to the frame

The middle strut makes the bend necessary for the onion shape

Three-piece struts – 16 in total – run from the drum to the top post

St. Basil's in Red Square peeps over the Kremlin

Beklemishev Tower defended the eastern approaches on the Moscow River

Overlapping tongued shingles, lemekhi, are made of aspen wood

Cross boarding links the vertical struts forming the frame

Drum, or base, of cupola

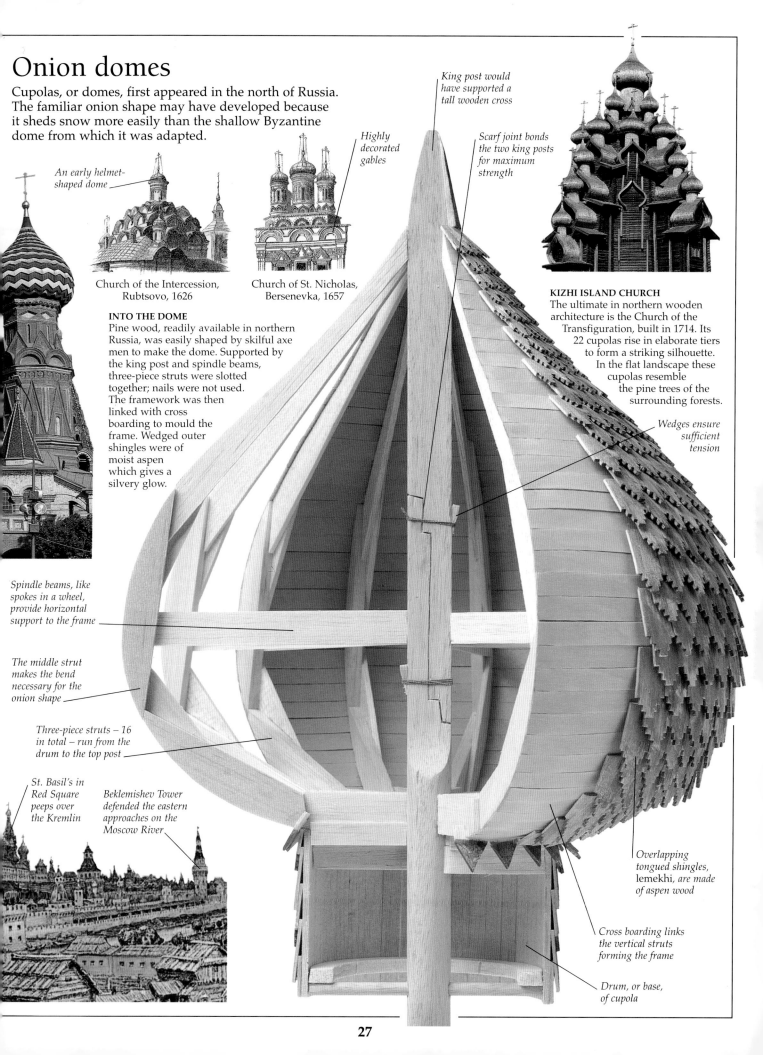

Palaces of St. Petersburg

ON THE MARSHY banks of the River Neva, Peter the Great built his new capital, St. Petersburg. He wanted to give Russia an outlet to the sea and a "window on the west". By 1712 the city had sprung into being but at the cost of thousands of lives. St. Petersburg is a place of palaces and spires, reflecting the European classical style of its many foreign architects. During World War II over one million inhabitants died as a result of a three-year blockade by the German army. St. Petersburg became Petrograd between 1914 and 1924, then Leningrad until 1991, when the original name was restored.

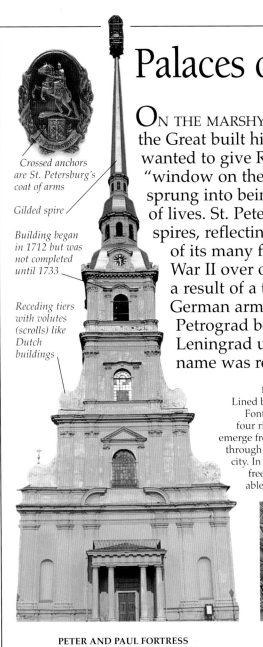

Crossed anchors are St. Petersburg's coat of arms

Gilded spire

Building began in 1712 but was not completed until 1733

Receding tiers with volutes (scrolls) like Dutch buildings

Alexander Column is a memorial to the 1812 victory over Napoleon

ARCHITECT RASTRELLI

Italian Bartolomeo Rastrelli (1700–71) was court architect under Empresses Anna and Elizabeth. He built stunning royal palaces of astonishing size and colour with lavish interiors. But his work fell out of favour with Catherine II, who preferred classical architecture.

FROZEN FONTANKA

Lined by grand houses, the Fontanka River is one of four rivers and canals that emerge from the Neva to loop through the centre of the old city. In winter the Fontanka freezes so hard that it is able to support vehicles.

CITY LAYOUT

St. Petersburg is grouped around narrow rivers and canals with the broad River Neva at the centre. Large islands like the Vasilievsky on the left and Hare Island where the fortress stands, face the mainland. Nevsky Prospekt is the most important of the streets that radiate south from the River Neva.

PETER AND PAUL FORTRESS

The fortress, begun in 1703, was the first construction built in the city. Rising from its centre is the Cathedral of Saints Peter and Paul. With its tall, slim spire, it is a symbol of the city as much as St. Basil's is of Moscow.

Top floor of the palace was used as servants' quarters

WINTER PALACE

The magnificent Winter Palace, completed in 1762 for Empress Elizabeth, is Rastrelli's crowning achievement. It is a closed square with a spacious courtyard built on the banks of the River Neva. It burned down in 1837 but within a year was rebuilt almost exactly as before. For long the main residence of the tsars, the Winter Palace became the Hermitage Museum after the Revolution.

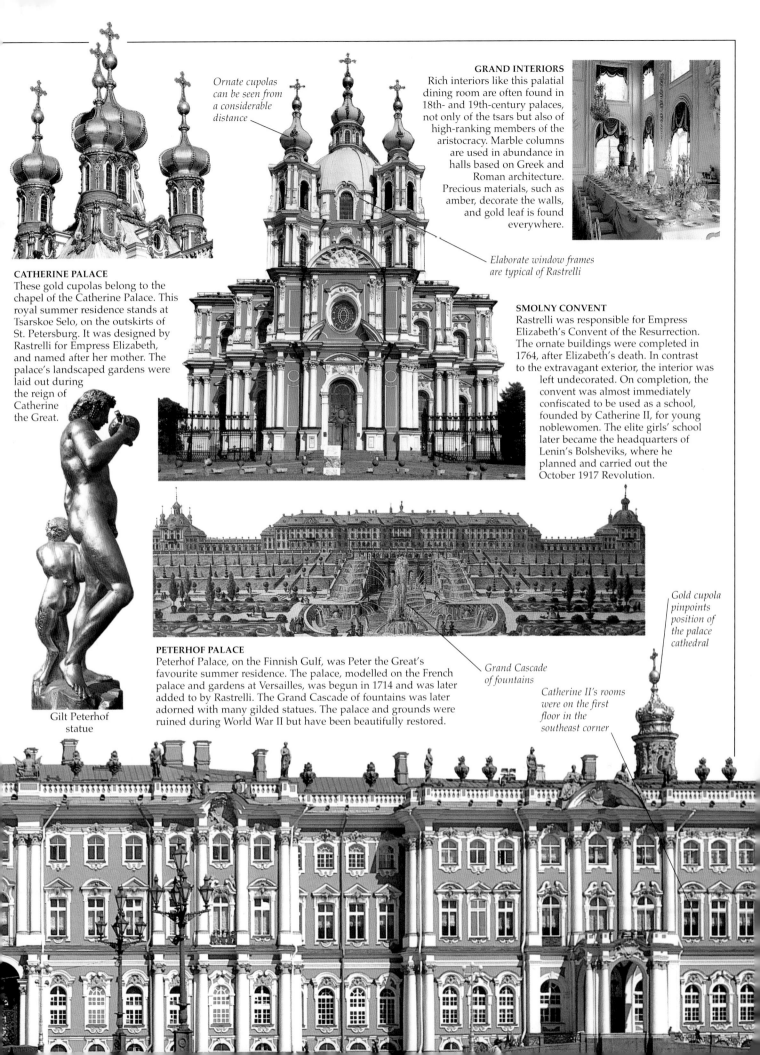

Ornate cupolas can be seen from a considerable distance

GRAND INTERIORS
Rich interiors like this palatial dining room are often found in 18th- and 19th-century palaces, not only of the tsars but also of high-ranking members of the aristocracy. Marble columns are used in abundance in halls based on Greek and Roman architecture. Precious materials, such as amber, decorate the walls, and gold leaf is found everywhere.

Elaborate window frames are typical of Rastrelli

CATHERINE PALACE
These gold cupolas belong to the chapel of the Catherine Palace. This royal summer residence stands at Tsarskoe Selo, on the outskirts of St. Petersburg. It was designed by Rastrelli for Empress Elizabeth, and named after her mother. The palace's landscaped gardens were laid out during the reign of Catherine the Great.

SMOLNY CONVENT
Rastrelli was responsible for Empress Elizabeth's Convent of the Resurrection. The ornate buildings were completed in 1764, after Elizabeth's death. In contrast to the extravagant exterior, the interior was left undecorated. On completion, the convent was almost immediately confiscated to be used as a school, founded by Catherine II, for young noblewomen. The elite girls' school later became the headquarters of Lenin's Bolsheviks, where he planned and carried out the October 1917 Revolution.

Gilt Peterhof statue

Gold cupola pinpoints position of the palace cathedral

PETERHOF PALACE
Peterhof Palace, on the Finnish Gulf, was Peter the Great's favourite summer residence. The palace, modelled on the French palace and gardens at Versailles, was begun in 1714 and was later added to by Rastrelli. The Grand Cascade of fountains was later adorned with many gilded statues. The palace and grounds were ruined during World War II but have been beautifully restored.

Grand Cascade of fountains

Catherine II's rooms were on the first floor in the southeast corner

Bolshevik Revolution

AFTER RIOTS in Petrograd (St. Petersburg until 1914) in February 1917, Nicholas II abdicated the throne and a Provisional Government took over. The Revolution had many causes. In 1905, widespread discontent erupted in strikes, uprisings, and mutinies. Food shortages, the tsar's weak leadership, and Russia's disastrous performance in World War I heightened unrest. Failure to stop the war angered soldiers and peasants, and in October 1917 the Bolshevik (Communist) Party, led by Vladimir Lenin, seized power. Lenin dissolved the Provisional Government and made peace with Germany at the cost of huge territories, including Ukraine.

GRIGORI RASPUTIN
The fake "holy man", Grigori Rasputin, gained huge influence over Nicholas II and Empress Alexandra due to his apparent ability to cure the haemophilia attacks of their son and heir, Alexei. While the tsar was at the front during World War I, Rasputin virtually ruled Russia. In 1916 the unpopular Rasputin was murdered by relatives of the tsar.

Peaceful demonstrators slain by tsar's troops

WORKERS UNITE
In Moscow, the 1917 Revolution was more violent than the almost bloodless coup in Petrograd. Militant workers fought fiercely against the stronger forces of cadets loyal to the Provisional Government. Only after ten days of furious fighting around the Kremlin did the Bolsheviks emerge triumphant in Russia's second capital.

Blank shots fired from the Aurora signalled the start of the Bolshevik uprising

"BLOODY SUNDAY"
On 9 January 1905, a young priest, Father Gapon, led workers from St. Petersburg's factories to the Winter Palace to petition the tsar. Hundreds of peaceful demonstrators, including women and children, were killed when soldiers opened fire. The massacre shook the nation's faith in the tsar.

WWI Russian troops wear gas masks while fighting in the trenches

WORLD WAR I
Russia, an ally of France and Britain, entered World War I in 1914. Russia's troops fought bravely and at first won important victories against Austria and Germany. But her armies lacked adequate supplies and later suffered defeats, with heavy losses and desertions. Popular enthusiasm gave way to disillusion and war-weariness.

SIGNAL FOR THE REVOLUTION
The sailors of the cruiser *Aurora* mutinied against their officers in March 1917 and joined the Bolsheviks. Anchored on the River Neva in central Petrograd, the *Aurora* fired a blank shot on 25 October 1917. The shot signalled the storming of the almost undefended Winter Palace where the remaining members of the Provisional Government were meeting.

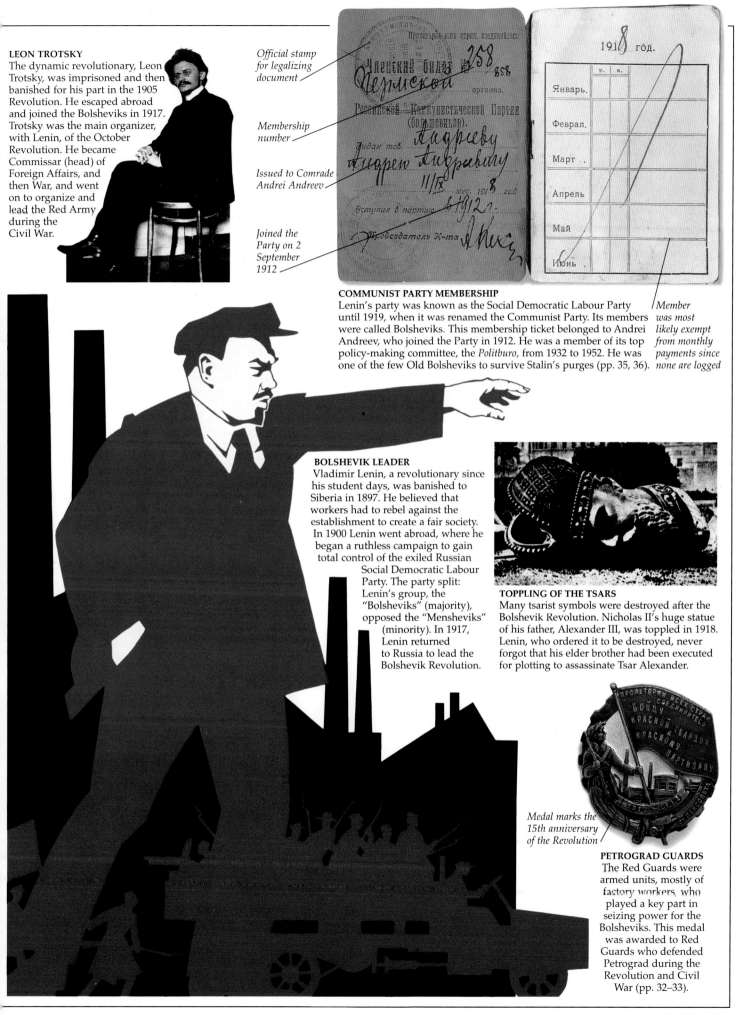

LEON TROTSKY
The dynamic revolutionary, Leon Trotsky, was imprisoned and then banished for his part in the 1905 Revolution. He escaped abroad and joined the Bolsheviks in 1917. Trotsky was the main organizer, with Lenin, of the October Revolution. He became Commissar (head) of Foreign Affairs, and then War, and went on to organize and lead the Red Army during the Civil War.

Official stamp for legalizing document

Membership number

Issued to Comrade Andrei Andreev

Joined the Party on 2 September 1912

COMMUNIST PARTY MEMBERSHIP
Lenin's party was known as the Social Democratic Labour Party until 1919, when it was renamed the Communist Party. Its members were called Bolsheviks. This membership ticket belonged to Andrei Andreev, who joined the Party in 1912. He was a member of its top policy-making committee, the *Politburo*, from 1932 to 1952. He was one of the few Old Bolsheviks to survive Stalin's purges (pp. 35, 36).

Member was most likely exempt from monthly payments since none are logged

BOLSHEVIK LEADER
Vladimir Lenin, a revolutionary since his student days, was banished to Siberia in 1897. He believed that workers had to rebel against the establishment to create a fair society. In 1900 Lenin went abroad, where he began a ruthless campaign to gain total control of the exiled Russian Social Democratic Labour Party. The party split: Lenin's group, the "Bolsheviks" (majority), opposed the "Mensheviks" (minority). In 1917, Lenin returned to Russia to lead the Bolshevik Revolution.

TOPPLING OF THE TSARS
Many tsarist symbols were destroyed after the Bolshevik Revolution. Nicholas II's huge statue of his father, Alexander III, was toppled in 1918. Lenin, who ordered it to be destroyed, never forgot that his elder brother had been executed for plotting to assassinate Tsar Alexander.

Medal marks the 15th anniversary of the Revolution

PETROGRAD GUARDS
The Red Guards were armed units, mostly of factory workers, who played a key part in seizing power for the Bolsheviks. This medal was awarded to Red Guards who defended Petrograd during the Revolution and Civil War (pp. 32–33).

The Civil War

THE COMPARATIVELY bloodless October Revolution (pp. 30–31) was followed by a cruel Civil War between the anti-Communist White Army and the Bolshevik Red Army. The White forces lacked strong leadership but, aided by Western powers, enjoyed early successes. In 1920, however, the Red Army, joined by many tsarist officers, was victorious. Although the Bolsheviks lost Poland, Finland, and the Baltic States, the rest of the Russian empire remained within the new Communist State. The horror of Civil War was followed by a terrible famine, relieved only by U.S. aid. In 1921, to restore the ruined country, Lenin announced the New Economic Policy. This reintroduced private trade.

WAR BOATS
River steamers like this one, rechristened *Vanya the Communist*, were taken over for use in the Civil War. The boat was destroyed in a fierce battle on the River Kama in October 1918.

Shield protects machine-gun operator from enemy bullets

Imperial
sword

Execution of Tsar Nicholas II

"*Workers of all countries unite! In struggle you will win justice!*"

Machine gun mounted on a former private carriage

SLAUGHTER OF THE ROMANOVS
In July 1918, the White forces threatened Yekaterinburg in Siberia, where the Bolsheviks were holding Nicholas II, the former tsar. Early on 17 July 1918, by Lenin's order, the tsar and his family were murdered. Their bodies, burned and buried in a pit in the forest, were not discovered until 1992.

WORDS OF MARX
This Bolshevik banner quotes the words of Karl Marx who, in his *Communist Manifesto* (statement of aims), urged the workers to unite since they had nothing to lose but their chains. After the October Revolution, however, power went not to the workers but to the Communist Party leaders.

Tsarist Imperial Army badge

WHITES AGAINST REDS
White Army soldiers were against the Communist takeover for a variety of reasons: some still supported the tsarist regime; some wanted the Provisional Government (p. 30) to be restored; while others were completely opposed to Bolshevik ideas.

RED ARMY TROOPS

The ill-disciplined voluntary Red Guards were transformed into the Red Army by the brilliant commander, Leon Trotsky. He appointed former tsarist officers and reintroduced order and distinctions between officers and soldiers. He kept close contact with the army by travelling quickly to areas of conflict in his armoured train.

Red Army cap badge, 1919

Flaps can be turned down to keep ears warm in winter

ARMY RECRUITMENT

Mass conscription (compulsory enrolment) meant that many army recruits came straight from the countryside with little or no military training. They were reluctant soldiers: many deserted the army and returned to their villages, especially at harvest time.

"I am a ploughman on guard, with my rifle I stand, I preserve freedom and my land".

DRESSED TO KILL

Red Army uniforms were haphazard affairs. Many soldiers wore their own clothes, or captured White uniforms, and crude birch-bark *lapti* shoes instead of boots. The pointed hat with the star, called a *budyonovka* after Marshal Budyonny, came to symbolize the Red Army soldier.

Sight aligns eye with target

MARSHAL BUDYONNY

This pistol belonged to Red Army commander Marshal Budyonny, a former officer in the Imperial Cavalry. His skilled horsemanship in battle became legendary.

Order of the Red Banner, 1921

RED COMMISSAR

Commissars were Party members attached to Red Army units to ensure political loyalty. They carried arms and were better dressed than most army members.

Seat for soldiers

Document case for paperwork

Carriage was drawn by horses

Metal-rimmed wooden wheels made it difficult to manoeuvre the carriage on rough terrain

CIVIL WAR CARRIAGE

The *tachanka*, a horse-drawn carriage with mounted machine gun, is typical of the makeshift methods of the chaotic Civil War. This *tachanka* was employed in a famous battle in which Germans, Poles, and Ukrainian nationalists fought for control of the Ukraine before the Reds finally won in 1920.

The rise of Stalin

LENIN DIED IN 1924 and the struggle began to inherit the leadership of the Communist Party. Trotsky, the most able candidate, was soon outmanoeuvred by Joseph Stalin, the devious secretary general of the Party. Stalin joined with two other leaders to defeat Trotsky then formed a new alliance to oust them as well. Trotsky was exiled in 1929. Stalin then strengthened his power by launching rapid industrialization and agricultural collectivization. The Great Terror began in earnest with the murder, in 1934, of the leading Bolshevik, Sergei Kirov. The secret police, the NKVD (later the KGB) became all-powerful, directing mass arrests from their infamous headquarters in Moscow. All the famous Old Bolshevik leaders were tried or shot.

DESTRUCTION OF CHURCHES
Churches were not only closed but, by the late 1920s, began to be destroyed in large numbers. The massive Cathedral of Christ the Saviour (p. 58) in Moscow was completed in 1883 as a memorial to the Russian victory over Napoleon. It was blown up in a huge explosion in 1931 to make way for the Palace of the Soviets (see below).

This 1920s cartoon reflects Lenin's wish to convert the world to Communism

LENIN AND WORLD REVOLUTION
This cartoon of Lenin sweeping the world clean of priests, capitalists, and kings illustrates the Communist hope that the Revolution would spread around the world. But Communism was not successful abroad. At home Lenin persecuted merchants, monarchists, and priests, closed churches, and nationalized trade and industry.

LENIN'S FUNERAL TRAIN
When Lenin died in January 1924, his body was brought to Moscow by train for a huge public funeral. His body was embalmed (preserved), placed in a specially built mausoleum (tomb) in Red Square, and exhibited to the public. The mausoleum also served as a platform for Soviet leaders viewing the annual parades on May Day and 7 November (pp.56–57).

Train was made at the Putilov factory in St. Petersburg, 1910

Renovated in 1923, the train became a memorial to Lenin in 1937

ШГ БЕСПАРТИЙНЫХ
КОММУНИСТАМ

Р.У. ж.д. У.127

MONUMENTAL PALACE
This design for the Palace of the Soviets was drawn in the 1930s. It was to be the tallest building in the world. But only the foundations were laid since building problems and World War II halted construction.

Motherhood award could be attached to a chain and worn proudly as a necklace

MOTHERHOOD AWARDS
After the Bolshevik Revolution, the government supported women's freedom, but by the 1930s traditional roles of women as wives and mothers were emphasized. To encourage a higher birth rate, the Motherhood Medal was granted to women with five children; those producing ten were declared Heroine Mothers.

RULE OF STALIN
Joseph Stalin became leader after Lenin's death by outmanoeuvring Trotsky, Lenin's natural successor, and other leaders. In the late 1920s he introduced forced collectivization of agriculture and rapid industrialization, which brought many hardships. Freedom of thought in the arts was also suppressed. Any remaining opposition was eliminated in the mass purges of 1937 (p. 36).

Hammer and sickle were adopted as emblems of the new State

COLLECTIVE FARMING
Collective farms combined small holdings into single units, often including several villages. Despite the invitation on this poster, peasants had no choice. In 1929 Stalin launched forced collectivization. The peasants resisted and millions died, or were shot or sent to labour camps. Production fell, causing a terrible famine. By 1938 collectivization had spread throughout the Soviet Union.

"Come to us in the collective farm!"

Soviet children were cared for in State crèches while their mothers worked

Stalin's real name was Dzhugashvili. Stalin comes from "stal", the Russian for steel; he adopted it while he was working secretly for the early Bolsheviks

WOMEN'S ROLE
The new Soviet state granted women full legal equality. But by the 1930s the State became more authoritarian and women were expected to perform a dual role. They had not only to cook, clean, and shop for the family, but also do heavy manual labour on the farms or in the new factories. Childcare was organized to release women for work outside the home, but poor housing and lack of amenities made their lives arduous.

Stalin's moustache, simple clothes, and high leather boots were copied by the other leaders

Soviet Russia

DURING STALIN'S PURGES millions of innocent people were executed or sent to remote labour camps (*gulags*). These horrors were followed by the hardships of World War II. When the Soviet Union was invaded, Moscow nearly fell to the Germans and Leningrad suffered a long siege. After the war, good relations with Western allies deteriorated and the Cold War began. After Stalin's death in 1953, relations began to improve. But Khrushchev's dangerous Cuban missile crisis sent relations into decline again. It was not until Gorbachev became Party leader in 1985, and introduced the policies of *glasnost* (freer speech) and *perestroika* (reform) that relations improved considerably.

GERMAN INVASION
Breaking the Nazi-Soviet peace pact, Germany invaded the Soviet Union in June 1941. Stalin and the Red Army were taken by surprise and much of the western Soviet Union was occupied. But the Germans were turned back from Moscow, defeated at Stalingrad on the Volga in 1943, and pushed back to Berlin. They finally surrendered at Reims, France, on 7 May, 1945. Two days later, Red Army soldiers gathered in front of the mausoleum (tomb) in Red Square, Moscow, and threw captured Nazi flags before Stalin and other leaders.

Dzherzhinsky, founder of the Cheka, *the Soviet secret police*

Mass grave marking from a gulag *near Karaganda in Central Asia*

LABOUR CAMPS
Wooden grave tablets recorded only the burial sites – no prisoner names or numbers – of those who died in Stalin's labour camps (*gulags*). An estimated 20 million people were swallowed up in the huge concentration camp system.

STATE UNIVERSITY
The old Moscow University was expanded in Soviet times, and a large new university building was erected in the Lenin Hills. The building is one of Stalin's seven ornate, tiered skyscrapers, which changed the face of Moscow in the early 1950s. They are popularly known as wedding-cake palaces.

Constructed 1949–53, the central tower is 35 storeys high

The vast building contains not only departments and lecture halls but living quarters for the staff and students

Building's lower wings extend out from the centre in U shapes

FOUNDER OF THE SECRET POLICE
Felix Dzerzhinsky was the first head of the Soviet secret police, then called the *Cheka*, after the 1917 Revolution. His hated statue (above), which stood on Lubyanka Square opposite the KGB headquarters in Moscow, was pulled down after the failed coup of 1991 (pp. 58–59). It now stands in a sculpture park in Moscow, along with statues of other leaders of the rejected Soviet regime.

CUBAN MISSILE CRISIS
In 1962, during the long Cold War (period of hostility between western countries and the Soviet Union), Soviet leader Nikita Khrushchev placed missiles in Cuba, within range of U.S. cities. Cuba, a Communist state ruled by Fidel Castro, was a strong supporter of the Soviet Union. U.S. President John F. Kennedy immediately ordered a naval blockade of Cuba. Six days later Khrushchev backed down; the missiles were removed. A war had only just been avoided. The Communist Party's Central Committee forced Khrushchev to retire in 1964.

CONTROLLING THE ARTS
Under Stalin, writing, art, and even music had to praise Communism, Soviet life, and Stalin himself. *Worker and Peasant*, a sculpture by Vera Mukhina, was made for an exhibition in Paris in 1937.

Worker and the Peasant, "looking into the glorious Communist future", was used as the symbol for Mosfilm, *the large Soviet film studio*

Sickle symbolizes the agricultural worker

Hammer signifies the factory worker

SOVIET SYMBOLS
Favourite themes for Soviet emblems were sheaves of wheat and the hammer and sickle used to decorate railings on one of Moscow's bridges. Portraits of the Party leader, hung on the walls of every office and institution, were changed when that leader fell out of favour. Instead of advertising, huge Party slogans decorated city streets and buildings.

The figures, made of stainless-steel panels, are young, strong, and attractive

Anniversary meeting of the Bolshevik Revolution took place here in 1941, as bombs fell outside during World War II

MOSCOW METRO
The construction of the Moscow underground was one of the engineering feats of the Stalin era. Its ornate stations were referred to as "palaces for the people". The first line opened in 1935 and each marble-lined station was decorated with sculptures or mosaics displaying a different theme. Most large cities in Russia now have a metro system. One of the most beautiful stations is Mayakovskaya (above).

Rail and industry

ALTHOUGH A LATE starter, by 1914 Russia had become the fifth largest industrial power in the world. After the Revolution and Civil War, production of manufactured goods fell sharply but rose again when Stalin launched his Five-Year Plans. However, tight government control left little room for new ideas, and Soviet Russia fell behind other modern economies. Industry was in crisis when the Soviet Union broke up in 1991, and production fell further when the new government moved abruptly to a market economy. In such a large country the railway network is vital. The first line, from Tsarskoe Selo to St. Petersburg, opened in 1837. By 1899 it had been extended east, greatly helping to open up the vast mineral wealth of Siberia.

"...TO WORK, COMRADES!"
Propaganda posters called on people to throw themselves into the work of the new factories. In 1928 Stalin announced the first Five-Year Plan under which rapid expansion of heavy industry was to be achieved by setting monthly and annual targets. In spite of tremendous hardships, by 1937 the Soviet Union had become the second largest industrial nation in the world.

Powerful lights enabled farmers to work through the night

Only the first tractors were fitted with wheel studs; later ones used caterpillar treads

COLLECTIVE FARMING
Industry was harnessed to manufacture mineral fertilizers and farm machinery to meet the needs of the new collective and State farms. Traditional wooden farming implements (pp. 16–17) were cast aside in favour of modern machinery.

Early Soviet tractors ran on diesel and were deliberately large for the enormous fields

FIRST SOVIET TRACTOR
This is the first tractor to roll off the production line of the Soviet Union's earliest tractor factory which opened in 1930. Farm machinery was not kept on the farms but at district Machine and Tractor Stations (MTS's), which decided when and where they would be used. Until they were scrapped in 1957, MTS's kept the farms under tight political control.

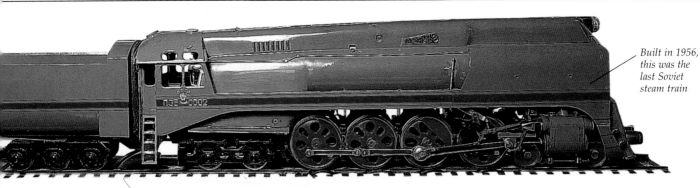

Built in 1956, this was the last Soviet steam train

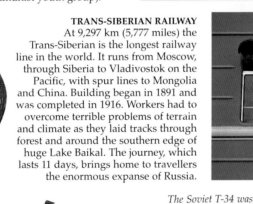

LAYING THE TRACKS
Russia's first railways were laid by thousands of workers using little more than pickaxes. During World War I, German prisoners of war built the important line to the ice-free port of Murmansk in the far north. The new line in eastern Siberia, the Baikal-Amur Magistral (BAM), completed in the 1980s, was built largely with volunteer labour by members of the *Komsomol* (Communist youth group).

PASSENGER TRAINS
Russian trains are all electrified or use diesel engines. They have a wider gauge (track width) than European trains; the carriages – especially the sleeping cars – are more spacious but cause problems at border crossings where the undercarriages have to be changed. There are no rapid trains as in Europe. The 650-km (404-mile) journey from Moscow to St. Petersburg takes five hours by express train.

RAILS ON PERMAFROST
It is very difficult to lay railway lines in northern and eastern Russia, where the layer of permafrost (p. 11) can be 1 km (0.62 miles) thick and the earth unstable during the short summer thaw. Nevertheless, rails have been successfully built beyond the Arctic Circle. They run as far as the coal-mining settlement at Vorkuta and the copper and nickel mines at Norilsk, where Stalin's concentration camps supplied forced labour between the 1930s and 1950s.

TRANS-SIBERIAN RAILWAY
At 9,297 km (5,777 miles) the Trans-Siberian is the longest railway line in the world. It runs from Moscow, through Siberia to Vladivostok on the Pacific, with spur lines to Mongolia and China. Building began in 1891 and was completed in 1916. Workers had to overcome terrible problems of terrain and climate as they laid tracks through forest and around the southern edge of huge Lake Baikal. The journey, which lasts 11 days, brings home to travellers the enormous expanse of Russia.

УЛААНБААТАР — МОСКВА

The Soviet T-34 was regarded as the best tank of World War II

Tank is painted white for camouflage in the snow

MASS-PRODUCED WEAPONS
At the start of World War II, hundreds of factories were moved east to the Urals and Siberia, beyond the reach of the invading German army. Tractor factories were adapted to produce tanks, such as the Soviet T-34, which played a big part in Russia's victory. After the war, Soviet industry continued to mass-produce weapons – over 20 per cent of the country's budget went on defence. In the new Russia, military spending has declined.

Kapitza's lenses

Science pioneers

RUSSIA HAS A LONG record of outstanding scientific achievement. In the 19th century Russian scientists made important advances in chemistry, radiotelegraphy, and mathematics. In the Soviet era priority was given to military science and space technology but political interference and unjustified arrests of scientists stifled progress. In 1980 Andrei Sakharov, whose theories enabled the Soviets to build a hydrogen bomb, was exiled for defending human rights. Russia was the first country to send an artificial satellite, and then a person, into space.

Living quarters on this model spaceship are above – control rooms below

Distillation jar used in experiments by Lomonosov

FATHER OF AVIATION
Nikolai Zhukovsky (1847–1921) is often called the "father of Russian aviation". In the early days of flying he began the study of aerodynamics. In 1905, he worked out how to calculate the lifting power of an aeroplane: later, he developed the whirlwind theory on which helicopter flight is based.

ATOMIC THEORIST
Mikhail Lomonosov (1711–65) was the greatest scientist of his day. A pioneering chemist and physicist, he anticipated part of the atomic theory two centuries before it was fully described. He was also a fine poet, and founder of Moscow University.

PAVLOV'S SALIVATING DOGS
As a physiologist, Ivan Pavlov (1849–1936) studied the brain, the nervous system, and digestion. By repeatedly sounding a bell at meal times, he trained a dog to salivate at the sound of the bell, rather than at the arrival of food. Through this study, Pavlov developed the theory of conditioned reflexes, which he later applied to humans. He won a Nobel Prize in 1904.

Metal filings in the coherer detect electrical waves and send signals via wires to coils

FIRST RUSSIAN RADIO
Alexander Popov (1859–1905), a physicist, invented the antenna (aerial). In 1895 he made his first radio (right) on which a message could be sent via an antenna to a receiver – it still works. The invention greatly improved communications between ship and shore, and assisted in the development of the telephone. Also, telegrams could now be sent by radio waves instead of over cables. Italian physicist, Guglielmo Marconi, who knew of Popov's experiments, patented a radio at about the same time.

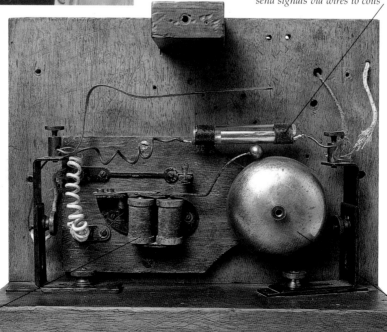

Electrical coils connect to a large battery at the back

VISIONS OF SPACE TRAVEL
Schoolteacher Konstantin Tsiolkovsky (1857–1935) was regarded as a dreamer for imagining space travel nearly a century before it happened. In 1903 Tsiolkovsky designed this spaceship and correctly wrote the theory of rocket power. In the 1920s, Tsiolkovsky developed the idea of jet engines, and proposed that rockets propelled by liquid fuel could be used to send ships into space. However, the technology that would make space travel a reality was not yet available.

Bell sounds when tapped by the stimulated electrical coils

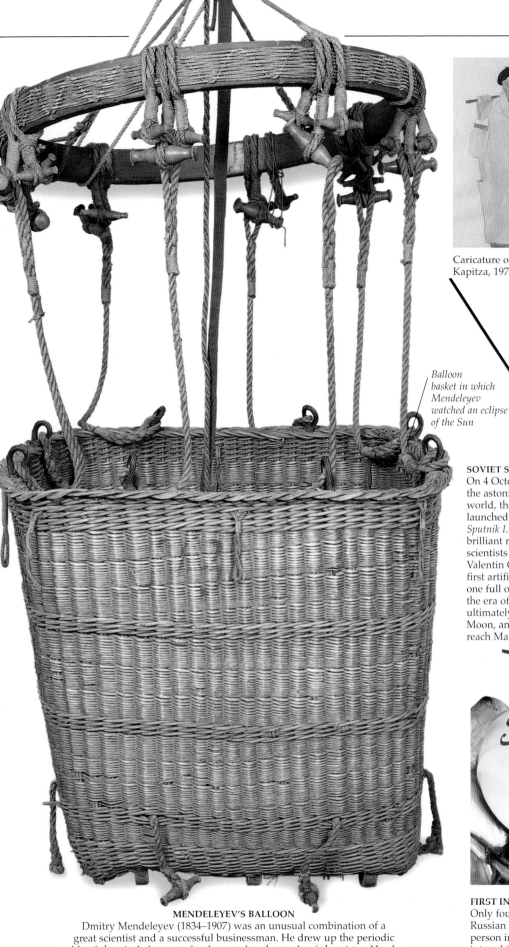

KAPITZA'S PHYSICS
Physicist, Pyotr Kapitza (1894–1984), won a Nobel Prize in 1978 for his work on low-temperature physics. Kapitza worked in England in the 1920s and 1930s. On a visit home in 1934, Stalin made him stay in the Soviet Union. From 1946 until Stalin's death, Kapitza was held under house arrest for refusing to work on the atomic bomb. But he kept up his research using handmade apparatus.

Caricature of Kapitza, 1971

This tiny thermos could hold liquid helium at the low temperatures needed for Kapitza's research

Balloon basket in which Mendeleyev watched an eclipse of the Sun

Four extendable aerials protrude from aluminium sphere

SOVIET SATELLITE
On 4 October 1957, to the astonishment of the world, the Soviet Union launched into space *Sputnik I*. Designed by the brilliant rocket and engine scientists Sergei Korolev and Valentin Glushko, *Sputnik* was the first artificial satellite, and made one full orbit of the Earth. It began the era of space exploration which ultimately saw people on the Moon, and unmanned probes reach Mars, Venus, and Jupiter.

Aluminium sphere contains a radio transmitter

MENDELEYEV'S BALLOON
Dmitry Mendeleyev (1834–1907) was an unusual combination of a great scientist and a successful businessman. He drew up the periodic table of chemical elements, fundamental to the study of chemistry. He also did pioneering work in crystallography, and on petroleum, gases, and liquids. Among his main interests were meteorology and astronomy. When an eclipse of the Sun occurred over Russia in 1887, Mendeleyev went up alone in this balloon basket to closely observe and take notes on the phenomenon.

FIRST IN SPACE
Only four years after the launch of *Sputnik I*, the Russian Yuri Gagarin (1934–68) became the first person in space. On 12 April 1961, he was launched into orbit aboard the capsule *Vostok I*, and made one circuit of the globe in 1 hour and 48 minutes before ejecting from the capsule and returning to Earth by parachute. Gagarin died a few years later when his jet plane crashed during a training flight.

Media and communications

CONTEMPORARY RUSSIAN USES the Cyrillic alphabet, which was developed in the 9th century to provide a written language for Slavic people. Largely based on the Greek script, Cyrillic also shares many letters with the Latin alphabet. The first Russian book was printed in 1563. Shortly afterwards, moralizing tales in comic-strip form (*lubok*) were printed. These were the earliest form of popular broadsheets, and remained popular until the 19th century. At the beginning of the 20th century, as more people learned to read, regular newspapers became common and book publication greatly expanded. Soviet Russia made great efforts to develop radio, cinema, and television – partly because of their value in spreading State propaganda.

POSTAL SYSTEM
Russia had a primitive postal system as early as the 13th century. By the 17th century it was better organized, with post stations providing fresh horses at stages along major routes. In 1874 Russia joined the International Postal Union. The modern system serves the whole vast country using air, rail, and water transport.

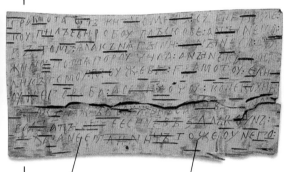

BIRCH-BARK TABLET
By the 13th century the northern city-state of Novgorod enjoyed a high standard of literacy, and even a form of democracy. Paper was not yet in common use, so messages were sent on pieces of birch bark, such as this one which conveys greetings to a citizen of Novgorod. These ancient letters were dug up by archaeologists from the University of Moscow in 1960.

Although buried for centuries, the writing is still legible

Birch bark is flattened for a smoother writing surface

Amplifier for broadcasting sound

Large wooden box containing receiver circuits

А	Б	В	Г	Д	Е
Ё	Ж	З	И	Й	
К	Л	М	Н	О	
П	Р	С	Т	У	Ф
Х	Ц	Ч	Ш	Щ	
Ъ	Ы	Ь	Э	Ю	Я

CYRILLIC SCRIPT
The Russian alphabet is known as Cyrillic after St. Cyril. He and his brother, St. Methodius, adapted the Greek alphabet in the 9th century to provide a written language for Slavic people. Cyrillic has 33 letters to match all the vowels and consonants used in Russian speech. This means the language is written just as it is spoken, and is very easy to spell and pronounce correctly.

НЕГРАМОТНЫЙ тот-же **СЛЕПОЙ**
ВСЮДУ ЕГО ЖДУТ НЕУДАЧИ И НЕСЧАСТЬЯ.

PROMOTING LITERACY
Before the reforms of Alexander II (p. 17), most Russians could not read or write. The opening of new schools meant that by 1917 over 40 per cent of the nation was literate. This poster was part of the Bolshevik campaign of the 1920s to achieve 100 per cent literacy.

GOING TO PRINT
Ivan Fyodorov, who printed the first Russian book in 1563, was run out of Moscow by the scribes, who were afraid of losing their jobs. In the early years of the 20th century, as people became more literate, a great expansion took place in book and newspaper printing.

Knob for adjusting the picture

SPREADING THE WORD
The phototelegraph, a technological advance in 1975, meant newspaper proofs could be sent quickly to every major city for simultaneous printing. It aided the centralized Soviet system as Party and government newspapers could appear at the same time in every city of the Soviet Union.

Viewing screen is just 3 cm (1.18 in) wide

On/off button

Volume control

COMMUNIST NEWS
The increase in literacy at the beginning of the 20th century led to the widespread availability of newspapers. *Pravda* began publication in a very small way in 1912 but reached a circulation of over 5 million during the Soviet period. Although its name means "truth", *Pravda* reported only what the Communist Party wanted the people to know, and real facts were often ignored or distorted. The main mouthpiece of the Communist Party, the newspaper has survived in the new Russia but with a much reduced circulation.

EARLY TELEVISION
In 1931 the first Soviet television set was produced, with only a tiny round screen. Transmissions began that year and by 1938 regular programmes were being broadcast in Moscow and Leningrad. But it was not until the 1960s that television became available throughout the entire country. Like other areas of Soviet life, television was highly controlled and focused on the capital, with the same programmes being relayed nationwide.

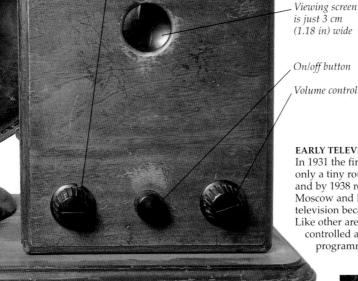

DOCUMENTING HISTORY
Sergei Eisenstein's films of the 1920s and 1930s are among the world's greatest. The scene above is from *October* (1927), about the Bolshevik Revolution. Under Stalin, film making was heavily controlled but after his death exceptional films appeared again. These included Andrei Tarkovsky's *Andrei Rublev* (1966), about a famous icon painter, and Tengiz Abuladze's *Repentance* (1987), which deals with Stalinist terror.

Famous writers

Russia's FIRST-RECORDED literature was the 12th-century heroic poem, *The Lay of Igor's Host* about the capture of a Russian prince. But it was in the 19th century that Russian writing became world-famous. Pushkin and Mikhail Lermontov wrote fine romantic poetry and stories. Gogol's biting stories, and the great novels of Tolstoy and Dostoevsky continued the Pushkin tradition. The last of the great 19th-century masters was Chekhov, who wrote brilliant plays and short stories. This great literary tradition continued in the 20th century with novels by Mikhail Bulgakov, Pasternak, and Solzhenitsyn, and the poetry of Anna Akhmatova and Osip Mandelshtam, as well as new works by women writers, such as Lyudmila Petrushevskaya and Tatiana Tolstaya.

Quill pen with which Gogol wrote Dead Souls

Script of Gogol's story, A Terrible Vengeance, *about a woman who falls under the spell of her father, a wizard*

NIKOLAI GOGOL
Gogol (1809–52) was a dramatist, novelist, and short story writer. His works were a mixture of fantasy, horror, and humour. Gogol wrote about Cossacks and of life in the Ukraine. But his greatest works were *The Government Inspector*, a play that made fun of provincial officials, and *Dead Souls*, a witty novel about serfs and landowners. Gogol burned his second volume of *Dead Souls* after a fanatical priest convinced him that the work was evil. Gogol died several days later, perhaps depriving the world of another masterpiece.

FYODOR DOSTOEVSKY
Dostoevsky (1821–81) is one of the world's greatest novelists but was often very poor. He was arrested in 1849 for association with a secret society and sentenced to death. While standing before the firing squad, Dostoevsky was pardoned and sent to Siberia. His terrible experiences are reflected in his account of prison life, *The House of the Dead*. He also wrote *Crime and Punishment*, a novel about a murder.

Silver tea strainer given to Pushkin by his nanny

ALEXANDER PUSHKIN
Pushkin (1799–1837) is considered to be Russia's greatest poet. He was exiled in 1824 for revolutionary and anti-religious writings. While in exile, Pushkin was looked after by his nanny, about whom he wrote the poem "*Companion in my Austere Days*". Among his greatest works are: the historical play, *Boris Godunov*; a long poem, *The Bronze Horseman*, about a tragic flood in St. Petersburg; and many wonderful lyrical poems which most Russians know by heart. Pushkin died, aged 37, fighting a duel, like the one in his greatest work, *Evgeny Onegin*, against one of his beautiful wife's admirers.

ANTON CHEKHOV

Chekhov (1860–1904), the grandson of a serf, was trained as a doctor but became a full-time writer. He was a master of the short story, some highly comic, others touching accounts of people's dreary lives. One of the best is *Lady with a Dog*, set in the resort of Yalta, where Chekhov, suffering from tuberculosis, lived for a time. Chekhov is best known for his great plays such as *The Seagull* and *The Cherry Orchard*.

Scene from the 1965 film *Dr. Zhivago*

Sculpture of Chekhov and the *Lady with a Dog*

Mandelshtam's satirical poem comparing Stalin to insects

BORIS PASTERNAK

During the long period of Stalin oppression, Pasternak (1890–1960) translated Shakespeare and Goethe. He won the Nobel Prize for his novel about the Civil War, *Dr. Zhivago*. Published abroad in 1957, it caused anger in the Kremlin and Pasternak was expelled from the Soviet Writers' Union.

The Cyrillic alphabet contains 33 letters

OSIP MANDELSHTAM

Among Russia's remarkable writers of the early 1900s was the gifted poet Mandelshtam (1891–1938) whose poems reflect great knowledge of the classical world. Banned from publishing in the 1930s, he was twice arrested and sent to the concentration camps. He died in Siberia in 1938, his crime a satirical poem about Stalin.

LEO TOLSTOY

Tolstoy (1828–1910) was a great novelist who wrote highly acclaimed novels, including the epic *War and Peace*, about Napoleon's invasion, and *Anna Karenina*, a tragic love story. He founded his own moral religion, based on Christianity, in which he rejected wealth. His ideas attracted followers from around the world, but he was attacked by the Church and State. He died at a railway station, aged 82, having fled from home after family disputes.

ALEXANDER SOLZHENITSYN

Solzhenitsyn (b. 1918) was arrested at the end of World War II for criticizing Stalin. His experiences are reflected in *One Day in the Life of Ivan Denisovich*. Published in 1962, it was the first story written about Soviet camp life.

Film still from *One Day in the Life of Ivan Denisovich* (1971)

Art and icons

In architecture, painting, and sculpture Russians throughout the ages have shown special feeling for colour and shape. Religious art (icons, frescoes, and mosaics) dominated until the 17th century, when other subjects – portraits and landscapes – became popular. In the 19th century the Wanderers (a society of artists who portrayed the realities of life), led by Ilya Repin, painted ordinary people and scenes from Russian history. In the early 1900s, Mikhail Vrubel's unique style of painting influenced modern artists like Malevich, Kandinsky, and Chagall. At first vivid and daring, Soviet art was soon forced to portray positive images of Soviet life. Modern abstract art was forced underground but is free in the new Russia.

DISCOVERY OF BLACK GEORGE
The horse in the popular icon of St. George and the dragon is usually white, not black. This rare 14th-century icon was discovered in 1959 in a northern village near Arkhangelsk. It was being used as a shutter for a barn and was hidden by a thick layer of paint. The icon was spied as the shutter was being stripped for repainting. Moscow restorers carefully cleaned the shutter to reveal this delightful, well-preserved icon.

Pestle for grinding pigments to a fine powder

NATURAL PIGMENTS
Pigments (colours) used in icon painting are derived from the natural world. White comes from lead, black from ash. From clay comes ochre. Bright red is from vermilion, a mercury compound; gold occurs naturally.

HISTORY OF ICON PAINTING
In Byzantium, icons painted to set rules were usually solemn and severe. But in Russia icon painting gradually took on a gentler, more emotional character. Andrei Rublev (c. 1360–1430) was one of the greatest Russian icon painters. He composed this beautiful picture, *The Old Testament Trinity*, of God the Father, Son, and Holy Ghost as guests of Abraham.

Bright blue lapis lazuli *comes from silica rock*

Red ochre

Gold

Vermilion (cinnabar)

Ground *lapis lazuli*

Icon restoration

Restoration of ancient icons is a painstakingly slow process. In the past, darkened icons were repainted – the new image on top of the old. In Soviet times restorers devised methods of preserving each layer.

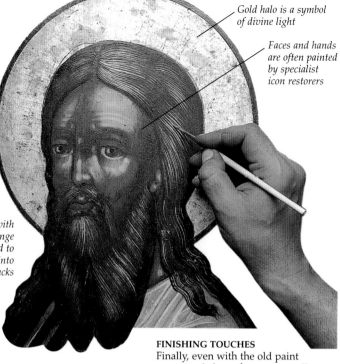

Gold halo is a symbol of divine light

Faces and hands are often painted by specialist icon restorers

Icons are blackened over time by candle smoke

Glue is applied with a brush; a syringe may be used to inject glue into surface cracks

STRENGTHENING
Icon is strengthened by soaking with fish glue until supple. Glued transparent paper is then ironed onto surface to stick down any peeling paint and left for up to six months.

CLEANING THE SURFACE
Glued paper is removed by wetting. After careful testing, the icon is cleaned with ether. It can take an hour or more to scrape away dirt from a small segment. Care is taken not to overlap a previously cleaned section. Oil and turpentine complete the cleaning.

FINISHING TOUCHES
Finally, even with the old paint secure and clean, there are usually fragments where the image has entirely disappeared. To repaint these sections, some Russian icon restorers use watercolours and not the egg tempera paint of the original artists. They want future restorers to know from the type of paint where the icon has been restored, and where the original painting has survived.

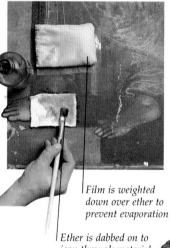

Film is weighted down over ether to prevent evaporation

Ether is dabbed on to icon through material

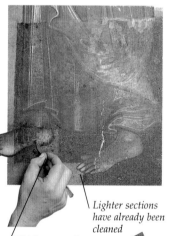

Lighter sections have already been cleaned

Dirt is removed carefully with a sharp knife

Rublev's figures, bowed in thought, are painted in soft, luminous colours

BEGINNINGS OF REALISM
Ilya Repin (1844–1930) came from a peasant family; he painted not only portraits but also controversial political and historical scenes. His *Religious Procession in Kursk* shows the poverty and blind faith of the people, and the hostility of the mounted police.

SOVIET ART
By the 1930s artists had to obey the Communist Party policy that all art should reflect a positive view of Soviet life. Stalin and other Soviet leaders were portrayed as wise and kind by artists like Alexander Gerasimov (1881–1963). His namesake, Sergei Gerasimov (1885–1964), in his *Collective Farm Festivities* presents a false view of jolly life on the farm. It was painted in 1937, the worst year of the Great Terror, when hundreds of thousands, including farmers, were arrested.

Malevich used these shapes in textile and pottery designs during the 1920s

ABSTRACT ART
The burst of creativity in Russia in all the arts at the beginning of the 20th century was reflected in the appearance of a modern abstract art. The uneducated but immensely talented Kasimir Malevich (1878–1935) experimented with colour, and geometric shapes to suggest force, motion, and space.

47

Music and dance

THE BUFFOON
A most original and witty composer of the 20th century, Sergei Prokofiev (1891–1953) wrote vivid and exciting music for the ballet *Romeo and Juliet*. This brilliant scenery was for his comic ballet *The Buffoon* (1915).

THE ORIGINS OF ST. PETERSBURG'S world-famous Kirov ballet go back to the 18th century. In 1776, the Moscow Bolshoi ballet began, using orphan children as dancers. At the end of the 19th century, French choreographer, Marius Petipa, created *Sleeping Beauty* and *Swan Lake*. These ballets were written to music by Tchaikovsky, the first of many great Russian composers, including Stravinsky, Prokofiev, and Shostakovich, to write for the ballet. From 1909 on, Sergei Diaghilev, founder of the Ballets Russes, sponsored radical ballets that burst like bombshells onto the world. The best new ballets of the Soviet era include *Romeo and Juliet*, *Spartacus*, and *The Golden Age*. Pavlova, Nijinsky, Ulanova, and Nureyev are some of Russia's greatest dancers.

DIAGHILEV'S GENIUS
Sergei Diaghilev (1872–1929), manager of the Ballets Russes, attracted talented composers, choreographers, and artists who together created outstanding ballets. He employed Mikhail Fokine as choreographer (creator of dance) to devise most of the company's famous ballets, including *Narcissus*. This brilliant costume for *Narcissus* was designed by Russian artist Leon Bakst, who excelled in the use of extravagant style and colour.

A SHOCKING COMPOSER
An original composer, Igor Stravinsky (1882–1971) shocked the public with his modern rhythms. He composed ballets for Diaghilev, such as the popular *Petrushka* (score sheet above). Stravinsky left Russia during World War I but his work continued to be inspired by Russian folk music.

"GOD OF DANCE"
After studying ballet, Vaslav Nijinsky (1889–1950) became a leading dancer of the Marinsky Theatre in St. Petersburg. He joined Diaghilev's Ballets Russes early and was not only dancer in such roles as *Petrushka* but also a choreographer. Many of the ballets owed their success to his legendary skill. But Nijinsky's relationship with Diaghilev deteriorated and by 1917 he had grown paranoid and withdrawn. From 1918 on, he spent his life in a mental hospital. His career had lasted just 10 years.

Nijinsky as Armida's page in *Le Pavillon d'Armide*

Pavlova dancing the Dying Swan

PRIMA BALLERINA
Anna Pavlova (1881–1931) was prima ballerina at St. Petersburg's Marinsky Theatre for several years before joining the Ballets Russes in 1909 and starring in Fokine's *Les Sylphides*. She finally left Russia during World War I and settled in London, where she formed her own small company. Pavlova was a superb classical ballerina with wonderful technique. She is shown here dancing in Tchaikovsky's *Swan Lake*.

REVOLUTIONARY BALLET

The *Rite of Spring* had music by Stravinsky, choreography by Nijinsky, and lyrics and costumes by the artist Nikolai Roerich. The wild drumming music was considered so outrageous at its first performance in Paris, in 1913, that a near riot broke out. The Paris performance, however, was followed by a successful London debut in the same year. *Rite of Spring* is now considered a landmark in 20th-century ballet.

Cap for a young man in the Rite of Spring *by Roerich*

PAGAN RUSSIA

The subject of the ballet, *Rite of Spring*, was pagan Russia before it became Christian. The ballet is divided into two parts: the first celebrates the adoration of the Earth, while in the second, a chosen maiden dances herself to death as a sacrifice to the Earth.

Squares, circles, waves, and dots are the basis of the design for the maiden's costume in the Rite of Spring

FOLK MUSIC

Russian folk music grew out of the the songs of the pagan Slavs. In medieval times, people sang epic ballads, playing a single-stringed instrument, *gusli*. The accordion has always been very popular among Russians, who love to sing when on holiday in the country, or at any gathering. Here, a 19th-century accordionist plays as peasants dance.

MUSICAL INSTRUMENTS

In early Russia the *domra*, a 3- or 4-stringed instrument with a rounded soundboard, and the *balalaika* with 3 strings and a triangular soundboard were popular. Among wind instruments the *rozhok* (shepherd's horn) and *dudka* (pipe) were played. The *balalaika* is still widely played, especially in villages and folk music bands.

The balalaika *normally has three strings and a fretted fingerboard*

The triangular soundboard is often painted with mythical figures

Crafts and traditions

IN THE PAST, THE ISOLATION of Russian villages and the long snowbound winters allowed peasants much free time to engage in craftwork. The abundance of wood encouraged carving; delightful wooden toys and domestic utensils, including the traditional drinking dippers (*kovsh*), were made in nearly every village. Some, like the colourful distaffs (*prialki*) for spinning, were brightly painted. Intricate embroidery and handmade lace are still produced in the northern towns. Icon painters, forbidden by the Bolsheviks in 1922 to pursue their craft, began to make lacquer boxes decorated with illustrations of fairy tales. Metal and pottery ware, and clay figurines also have a long tradition.

Brightly painted distaff is carved out of pine

Seat for spinner, who holds the board in place with her weight

SPINNING FLAX
Until recently, spinning and weaving took place in nearly every peasant home, and distaffs (*prialki*) were part of the essential household equipment. The women above, sitting on the porch of a large wooden house in northern Russia, are spinning flax using traditional distaffs.

COLOURFUL EMBROIDERY
In medieval times, when Russian women were confined to the home, they occupied themselves by establishing workshops. From these they not only fashioned their family's clothes but also embroidered elaborate cloths and robes for church purposes. Humbler people decorated their linen towels, wall hangings, and dresses with embroidery or drawn-thread designs of ancient origin. The 19th-century linen towel (above) embroidered with red thread (*kumach*) comes from the Vologda region, north of Moscow.

WOODEN SPINNER
The distaff, made of pine or birch, is a long board with a base on which the spinner sits. The wool or flax is held by the round projections at the upper end and pulled by the spinner to make a thread. Distaffs are usually gaily painted with designs of flowers or animals, or as here, the lion and the unicorn. It was common for a husband to present a distaff to his new bride.

DIPPING DUCK
In medieval Russia, the handled dipper (*kovsh*) was commonly used as a bowl for holding drinks. Dippers made from precious metals were often presented to important people by the tsars. The ancient form of the dipper is based on the shape of a duck or the prow of a boat.

This painted wood dipper, carved with a duck's head and tail, was made in the early 19th century

Wooden dippers are mostly made from pine but sometimes birch is used

Duck's head makes a useful handle to hold the bowl-like dipper

Brocade embroidered with gold thread

Mother-of-pearl geese and flowers decorate the headdress

GINGERBREAD TREAT

In Russian villages, crisp gingerbread was customarily baked in carved wooden moulds to celebrate weddings, funerals, and church holidays, and is still considered a great treat. The moulds have a long history, but by 1800 traditional designs of animals, birds, and the flowering bush – a sign of rebirth – began to change as new ideas from broadsheets, *lubok* (p. 42), with their cartoon-like illustrations became more widespread. This mould was made in the early part of the 19th century, and depicts a bearded peasant dressed up for a festive occasion.

Ribbons were tied in a large bow at the back of the head

The water carrier is a favourite subject among clay modellers

The cock is a popular figure in all types of Russian folk art

FESTIVE HEADDRESS

This beautiful bonnet (*kokoshnik*) comes from northern European Russia, near Arkhangelsk. Made at the end of the 18th century, it is open at the back which means it is for an unmarried girl: married women had to cover all their hair. Glass stones and mother-of-pearl are sewn on to a brocade background which is stiffened with canvas. The headdress would have been worn for weddings and other important festivals, and was handed down from mother to daughter.

CLAY FIGURINES

Homemade clay figurines were once part of a pre-Christian magic ritual, but by the 19th century were used as toys. They are still made at Dymkovo, now part of the city of Kirov, on the Vyatka River. The toys are shaped from potter's clay mixed with river sand. They are then fired, whitened with chalk, and painted in strong colours. The craft, which was dying at the end of the 19th century, was revived during the Soviet period.

Bread and salt are offered on an embroidered towel

Salt is placed in a pot or in a dent on the top of the loaf

Pink silk ribbons stream out at the back

BREAD-AND SALT-GREETING

Russians traditionally greet important guests by offering bread and salt on an embroidered towel held by the hosts' youngest daughter. The guest breaks off a piece of bread, dips it in salt, and eats it. Salt was considered such a luxury in old Russia that it was stored in a strong warehouse in Moscow on the *Solyanka*, or Salt Street. Russians are very hospitable to this day, and welcome and offer food to guests, however unexpected.

Childhood

CHILDREN ARE WELL LOOKED AFTER in Russian society. Crèches and nursery schools are provided for most mothers who work outside the home. Children start school aged 6 and can finish at the age of 14, or 16 if they go on to higher education. Some schools still use Soviet school uniforms which were similar to those of tsarist times – the girls wear brown dresses with white pinafores, the boys blue tunics and trousers. Soviet children belonged to organizations which emphasized Communist ideals. Children's literature and theatre are of a high quality in Russia.

BABY SWADDLING
It is customary in Russia to wrap babies up tightly in swaddling clothes for the first few months of life. Some people believe that this helps to straighten a baby's bones. Left swaddled for long periods of time, the babies are only occasionally released for a bath and a romp. Outside the hospitals, swaddling is gradually becoming less fashionable.

DRESSED LIKE MOTHER
This outfit from Orel province, southwest of Moscow, is typical of everyday wear for a little peasant girl in 19th-century Russia. It imitates her mother's clothes in that it consists of a sleeveless dress (*sarafan*) with a long-sleeved blouse underneath. The material is printed cotton, or calico, which would have been shop bought, rather than woven at home.

Felt boots are surprisingly waterproof on the ice

Strips of lace and other material decorate the skirt of the dress

OUTDOOR GEAR
Children need to dress warmly in the cold Russian winter. This little boy, gliding down an ice slide, wears a warm coat, scarf, mittens, a fur-lined *shapka* cap with flaps that can cover the forehead and ears, and felt boots, *valenki*, that are very warm in the snow.

WOODEN TOYS
Until the 20th century, Russian toys were made at home out of wood, the cheapest and most readily available material. Wood was made into puppets and all sorts of animals, from cows to bears. A favourite toy is the colourful *matryoshka* – peasant dolls which fit one inside the other.

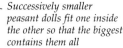

Successively smaller peasant dolls fit one inside the other so that the biggest contains them all

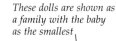

These dolls are shown as a family with the baby as the smallest

Children in Russia have a three-month summer holiday which allows many to enjoy the green countryside at a summer camp, or country home (*dacha*). This is an important respite from the crowded and noisy tower blocks of the city. Summer camps are organized through schools, or parents' places of work, and are often held in the country houses of the former nobles.

COMMUNIST YOUTH GROUPS

Nearly all Soviet children between the ages of 7 and 10 belonged to the Octobrists, those of 10 to 14 belonged to the Young Pioneers, and young people aged 14 to 28, the *Komsomol* (Young Communist League). These groups which taught loyalty to the Communist Party, also provided hobby clubs. In the 1930s, however, Soviet brainwashing of children was so intense that some even betrayed their parents to the authorities. After informing on his parents for helping *kulaks* (rich peasants), 14-year-old Pavlik Morozov's father was shot. Pavlik was then murdered by his angry uncle, but became a Soviet hero.

The bear is a favourite character in Russian fairy tales

Girl Pioneers wore a blouse and skirt and, like the boys, red scarves

CHILDREN'S LITERATURE

Russia is rich in children's literature. Traditional fairy tales (*skazky*) were collected and vividly illustrated in the early 20th century. They include the fantastic and terrifying witch *Baba Yaga*, who has iron teeth and lives in a hut which stands on chicken's legs. More recent children's writers are Samuel Marshak, author of fairy tales, and Kornei Chukovsky who wrote a Russian version of *Dr. Doolittle* called *Dr. Aibolit* (Dr. Ouchithurts).

SCHOOLS FOR THE GIFTED

Special schools were set up in the cities to encourage those talented in mathematics, languages, music, and sport. This little girl is studying dancing in a ballet school. Entry into the school is difficult and children have to show great talent. As well as learning the ballet, they follow the usual school lessons.

National pastimes

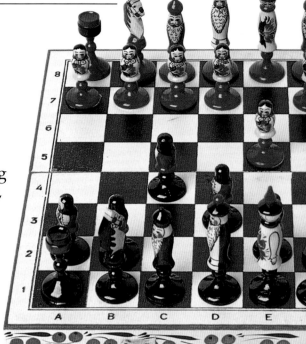

IN SUMMER, RUSSIANS enjoy swimming, countryside rambles, and fishing. Winter activities include skating, cross-country skiing, and fishing through ice holes. In autumn people of all ages love to go mushroom picking in the woods. Popular sports include soccer, ice hockey, at which Russia is a world leader, and tennis is rapidly gaining ground. Russians are also outstanding at gymnastics and perform well at many sports in the Olympics. Favourite games include chess and dominoes; older people can often be seen playing these in city parks. Even though most people have modern bathrooms, the weekly steam bath is still a regular event in both the city and the countryside.

CHESS CHAMPIONS
The game of chess came to Russia from China 1,000 years ago. After the 1917 Revolution, chess was strongly encouraged, and clubs were organized in schools and factories. Many recent world champions have been Russian.

Buckets of this sort are used in steam baths for washing, or to throw water on to the stove to create more steam

MUSHROOM PICKING
In the damp late summer and early autumn, thick clusters of mushrooms spring up in the woods and fields. Armed with baskets and buckets, people scour the countryside, and even city parks, for the many varieties of edible mushrooms. They take their trophies home to eat straight away, or to dry for future use.

Birch twig bunches for beating dirt out of one's pores are sold at the entrances to steam baths

COUNTRY REFUGE
In summer it is customary for city people to stay at a *dacha*, or country retreat. Children swim and play at the *dacha*, while adults fish, swim, tend the garden, walk in the woods, and enjoy a life in complete contrast to the bustle of the busy city.

STEAM BATHS
Russians delight in their weekly steam bath (*banya*). Many villages have their own steam baths, while in the cities they are found in every district. Busiest times are Friday and Saturday nights, the traditional time for a good scrub. People steam their bodies to extreme temperatures, lash themselves with birch twigs (*venik*), then plunge into a cold bath or, if in the countryside in winter, roll in the snow.

Dried mushrooms on strings last a long time and can easily be hung in the kitchen until needed

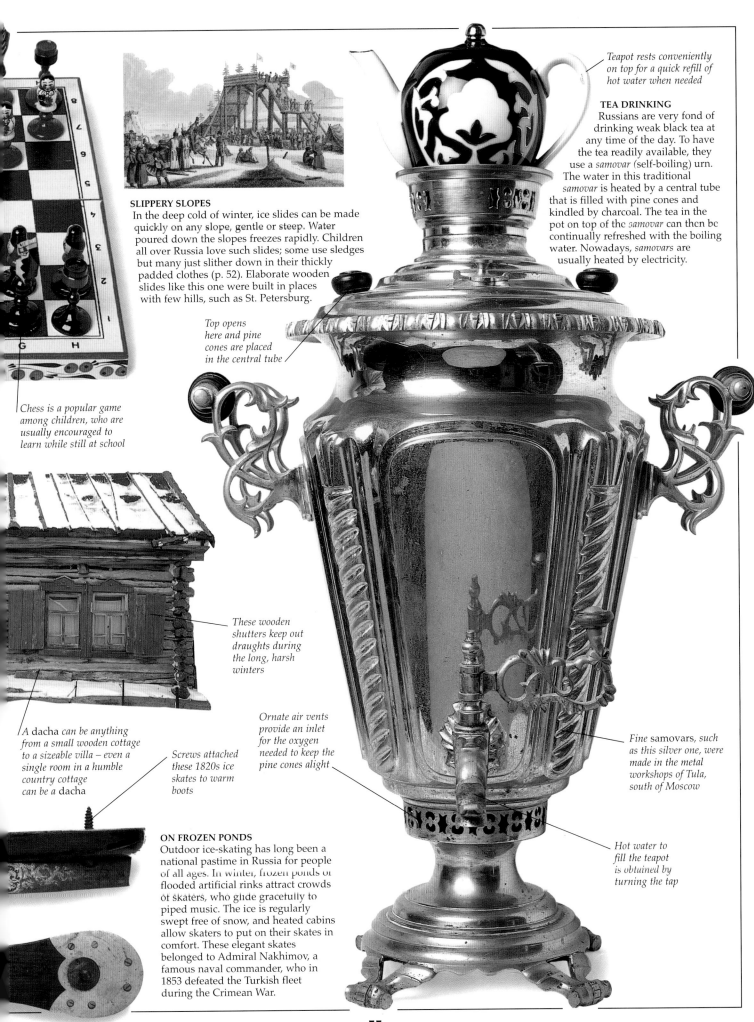

SLIPPERY SLOPES

In the deep cold of winter, ice slides can be made quickly on any slope, gentle or steep. Water poured down the slopes freezes rapidly. Children all over Russia love such slides; some use sledges but many just slither down in their thickly padded clothes (p. 52). Elaborate wooden slides like this one were built in places with few hills, such as St. Petersburg.

Chess is a popular game among children, who are usually encouraged to learn while still at school

These wooden shutters keep out draughts during the long, harsh winters

A dacha can be anything from a small wooden cottage to a sizeable villa – even a single room in a humble country cottage can be a dacha

Screws attached these 1820s ice skates to warm boots

ON FROZEN PONDS

Outdoor ice-skating has long been a national pastime in Russia for people of all ages. In winter, frozen ponds or flooded artificial rinks attract crowds of skaters, who glide gracefully to piped music. The ice is regularly swept free of snow, and heated cabins allow skaters to put on their skates in comfort. These elegant skates belonged to Admiral Nakhimov, a famous naval commander, who in 1853 defeated the Turkish fleet during the Crimean War.

Teapot rests conveniently on top for a quick refill of hot water when needed

TEA DRINKING

Russians are very fond of drinking weak black tea at any time of the day. To have the tea readily available, they use a *samovar* (self-boiling) urn. The water in this traditional *samovar* is heated by a central tube that is filled with pine cones and kindled by charcoal. The tea in the pot on top of the *samovar* can then be continually refreshed with the boiling water. Nowadays, *samovars* are usually heated by electricity.

Top opens here and pine cones are placed in the central tube

Ornate air vents provide an inlet for the oxygen needed to keep the pine cones alight

Fine samovars, such as this silver one, were made in the metal workshops of Tula, south of Moscow

Hot water to fill the teapot is obtained by turning the tap

Annual festivals

THE IMPORTANT FESTIVALS of the year in Russia begin with New Year which is celebrated like Western Christmas. Grandfather Frost and the Snow Maiden distribute presents, and on New Year's Eve families gather around a decorated fir tree for dinner and gift opening. Christmas is celebrated on 7 January because the Russian Orthodox Church observes the Julian calendar, which is 13 days behind the Gregorian calendar used elsewhere. Easter, the main religious festival of the year, even remained popular in Soviet times. Military parades on May Day and the anniversary of the Revolution have now ceased.

EASTER SERVICE
The long service begins late on the eve of Easter and continues through the night. At midnight the congregation, carrying lit candles, follows the priest; this symbolizes the women who came to the tomb of Christ and found it empty. At the doors of the church the priest proclaims, "Christ is risen". The worshippers joyfully reply, "He is risen indeed" and kiss their neighbours.

BREAKING THE FAST
As dawn breaks, the Easter service finishes and the worshippers disperse to their homes to break their long fast with special Easter foods and coloured eggs. The Easter cake, *kulich,* and the *paskha* (a sweet made of curd cheese) contain ingredients which were forbidden during Lent. Guests, who call continually all day, are offered the cakes.

Golden-domed monastery

On the side of the paskha is a cross, or "XB" which stands for "Christ has risen"

Men dress up in red robes and pass out pancakes to the crowds

CELEBRATION OF LENT
The eve of Lent is traditionally the time of the butter festival, *maslenitsa,* when pancakes are eaten in large amounts. With snow still thick on the ground, some hardy people celebrate by breaking holes in frozen lakes and rivers and diving into the icy water.

PAINTED EGGS
In the week before Easter everyone is busy painting eggs. Some are just boiled with onion skins, making lovely mottled brown and yellow colours. Others, with the yolk and white blown out through small pinholes in the end, are painted elaborately with religious or festive scenes. The eggs are eaten at the feast after the long Easter service.

This amusing painting shows a brown bear, one of Russia's national symbols, enjoying a sleigh ride

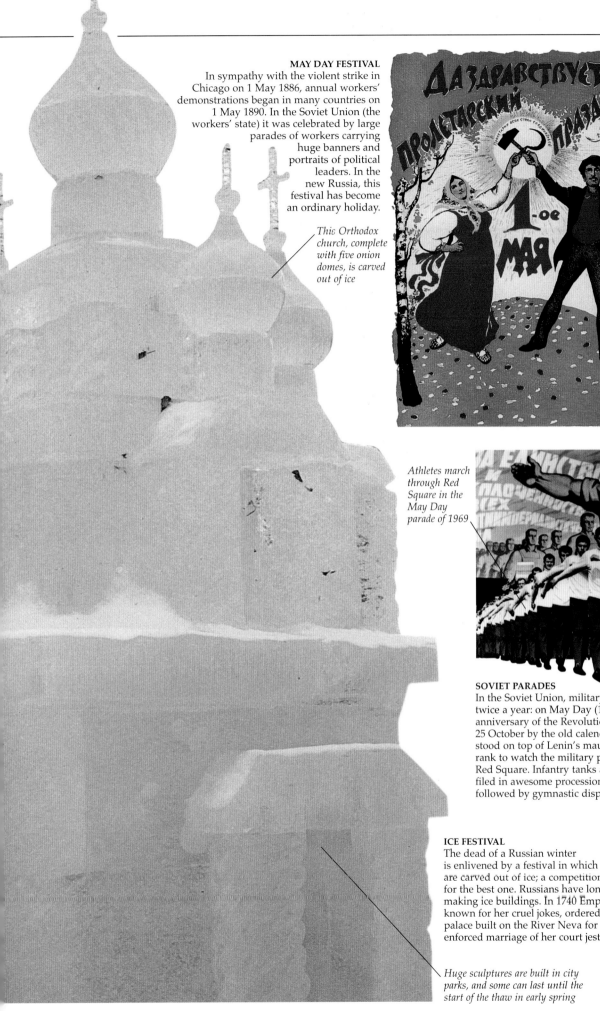

MAY DAY FESTIVAL
In sympathy with the violent strike in Chicago on 1 May 1886, annual workers' demonstrations began in many countries on 1 May 1890. In the Soviet Union (the workers' state) it was celebrated by large parades of workers carrying huge banners and portraits of political leaders. In the new Russia, this festival has become an ordinary holiday.

This Orthodox church, complete with five onion domes, is carved out of ice

"Long live the workers' festival"

Athletes march through Red Square in the May Day parade of 1969

SOVIET PARADES
In the Soviet Union, military parades were held twice a year: on May Day (1 May), and on the anniversary of the Revolution (7 November, or 25 October by the old calendar). Soviet leaders stood on top of Lenin's mausoleum in order of rank to watch the military parade pass through Red Square. Infantry tanks and giant rockets filed in awesome procession across the square, followed by gymnastic displays.

ICE FESTIVAL
The dead of a Russian winter is enlivened by a festival in which sculptures are carved out of ice; a competition is held for the best one. Russians have long enjoyed making ice buildings. In 1740 Empress Anna, known for her cruel jokes, ordered an ice palace built on the River Neva for the enforced marriage of her court jester.

Huge sculptures are built in city parks, and some can last until the start of the thaw in early spring

The new Russia

In August 1991 HARDLINE Communists staged a coup (overthrow) against President Gorbachev and his reforms. Newly elected president of the Russian republic, Boris Yeltsin, occupied the White House (Parliament building), in Moscow, in opposition to the coup. Moscow citizens rallied to Yeltsin's support and within three days the coup collapsed. At the end of 1991, the Soviet Union fell apart and the Russian Federation, led by Yeltsin, was born. In October 1993, Yeltsin dissolved the hardline parliament, which fiercely opposed his reforms. Again the White House was occupied, this time by Communists and nationalists. Yeltsin used force and about 150 people died, but the hardliners were defeated. Since then, Russia has kept moving towards a market economy. Despite crime and corruption, life is improving for many people.

NEW ECONOMY
In 1992 Russia attempted to change abruptly from a State-owned economy to a free-market system. At first there was confusion and huge price rises as the rouble (Russian currency) crashed in value. The economic reforms were then slowed down, and gradually the value of the rouble, which had never before operated in a free market, settled to about 8,000 to the British pound.

The Communist hammer and sickle flag came down on Christmas Day, 1991

In 1912, 500 roubles would be the annual salary of a tradesman

In the 1990s, 500 roubles can only buy one egg

Cathedral of Christ the Saviour was rebuilt in 1997 on its original site, where a swimming pool had stood since 1958

RESTORING THE PAST
Russian cities are taking on a fresh look as new businesses start and buildings are restored. Some important historic buildings destroyed during Soviet times, including the grand staircase of the Kremlin palaces, the Resurrection Gate on Red Square, and the Cathedral of Christ the Saviour (p. 34) have been rebuilt exactly as they were.

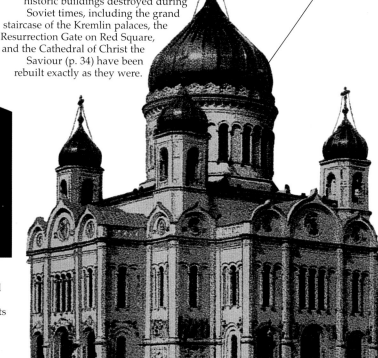

LAST LEADER OF THE SOVIET UNION
In 1985 the new Soviet leader Mikhail Gorbachev introduced a policy of openness (*glasnost*) followed by cautious reforms (*perestroika*). But he came under attack both from Communists opposing reform and radicals who wanted more democracy. After the failed coup of August 1991, Gorbachev was freed but found Yeltsin now in control and resigned four months later. But his reforms had made possible the new Russia.

OUT WITH THE OLD, IN WITH THE NEW

The four months from the August coup to 31 December 1991, were one of the most eventful periods in the history of Russia. In that time the Communist Party was dissolved, the republics that made up the Soviet Union broke away to form the loose grouping of the Commonwealth of Independent States (CIS), and Gorbachev, the last Soviet leader, resigned. On 25 December 1991, the red Soviet flag was lowered from the Kremlin. The new flag of Russia was raised in its place. The democratic Russian Federation was born.

New flag marked the end of Communism and the beginning of a democratic state

The red, white, and blue tsarist flag is now the flag of the Russian Federation

Estonia, Latvia, and Lithuania are collectively known as the Baltic States

Arctic Ocean

• Belarus

• Moldova   • Moscow
• Ukraine

Russian Federation

Republics of the
Caucasus   Republics of Central
Asia

Mongolia   China

POPULAR PRESIDENT

A construction engineer, Boris Yeltsin became Party boss in the Urals city of Sverdlovsk during the 1960s, and then of Moscow in the 1980s, under Gorbachev. He was sacked by Gorbachev in 1987. Four years later, however, he became president of the Russian republic, the largest of the Soviet republics. Yeltsin was the first Russian leader in history to be popularly elected. In democratic elections in June 1996, Yeltsin, although unwell, was re-elected president.

NEW RUSSIA

The Russian Federation, without the other 14 republics that made up the Soviet Union, is still the largest and potentially one of the most wealthy countries in the world. Of the 15 former Soviet republics, 12, including the Russian Federation, belong to the Commonwealth of Independent States (CIS). The Commonwealth's main aim is to promote economic and political co-operation between its members. The three remaining former Soviet republics – Lithuania, Latvia, and Estonia – have chosen not to join the Commonwealth of Independent States.

Index

A B C

Abuladze, Tengiz 43
agriculture 11, 13, 16, 23, 34, 35, 37, 38; tools 16, 17; machinery 38; MTS 38
Akhmatova, Anna 44
Alaska, sale of 23
Alexander I 23, 24
Alexander II 17, 21, 42
Alexander III 21, 31
Alexandra, Empress 21, 30
Andreev, Andrei 31
animals 10, 11; bear 10, 53; eagle 9, 21, 25; reindeer 10, 11, 13; tiger 10; wolf 11
Anna, Empress 28, 57
architecture 16, 18, 26–29, 34, 36, 46; Byzantine 27; Arctic 14, 15, 23, 39
armed forces: army 16, 20, 30, 32; Imperial Army, Cavalry 32, 33; navy 20, 22, 30, 32; recruitment 33
Armenia 12, 22
art 46–47; abstract 46, 47; religious 46, 47
arts, the 37, 42–47
Assumption Cathedral 24
Azerbaijan 12, 22
Bagration, General 22
Bakst, Leon 48
ballet/dance 48, 49, 53;
Baltic States 12, 22, 59
Batu 8, 9
Belarus/Belorussia 12, 23, 59
Billings, Joseph 23
Bloody Sunday 30
Bolsheviks 21, 24, 26, 29–32, 35, 42, 43, 50
books/literature 42–45, 53
bread and salt 51
broadcast media 37, 42, 43, 45; films 42, 43, 45
Budyonny, Marshal 33
budyonovka 33
Bulgakov 44
Buryat 12
Byzantium 8, 9, 18, 46
calendars 56
cartoons 34, 42, 51
Castro, Fidel 37
Cathedral of Christ the Saviour 34, 58
Catherine II (the Great) 16, 20, 21, 24, 25, 28, 29
Catherine Palace 14, 29
Caucasus 12, 15, 22, 59

Central Asia 12, 22, 36, 59
ceremonial robes 19
ceremonies 18, 24; coronation 24; marriage 18
Chagall, Marc 46
Chekhov, Anton 44, 45
children 35, 52–55;
Chukchi 11, 23
Chukovsky, Kornei 53
churches 27, 34; destruction of 34; of the Intercession 27; of St. Nicholas 27; of the Transfiguration 27
climate, winter 10, 11, 13, 16, 17, 28, 52, 55;
coats of arms 9, 11, 21, 28
collective farming 13, 34, 35, 47
commissars 33
communications 34, 40, 42–45, 51
Communist Manifesto 32
Communist Party 30–32, 34, 43, 47, 53, 58, 59
Communism 34, 37, 42, 43, 47, 53; propaganda 37, 38, 42, 43, 47; revolution 34
Convent of Resurrection 29
Cossacks 12, 16, 22, 23, 44
Crimea (Tauride) 9
Crown Jewels 20, 24
crowns 14, 18, 20, 24;
Cuban missile crisis 36, 37
Cyrillic alphabet 42

D E F G

dacha 53–55
Decembrist Revolt 20
Diaghilev, Sergei 48
Dmitry, Prince 9, 20
Dolgoruky, Prince Yury 26
Dostoevsky, Fyodor 44
Dzerzhinsky, Felix 36
Easter eggs 25, 55
economy, free-market 58
education 20, 52, 53
Eisenstein, Sergei 43
Elizabeth, Empress 21, 24, 28, 29
emancipation of serfs 17, 21
Fabergé, Peter Carl 25
fairy tales (*skazky*) 11, 50, 53
festivals 56, 57
fish/fishing 10, 13–15, 54; caviar/sturgeon 14, 15
Five-Year Plan 38
Fokine, Mikhail 48
food shortages 30, 32
forests 14, 15; taiga 11
fossil fuels 14, 15
fur trading/farms 14, 23
Fyodorov, Ivan 43
Gagarin, Yuri 41
Gapon, Father 30

Georgia 9, 12, 22
Genghis Khan 8, 9
Gerasimov, Alexander 47
Gerasimov, Sergei 47
gingerbread 51
glasnost 36, 58
Godunov, Boris 20, 44
Gogol, Nikolai 44
Gorbachev, Mikhail 36, 58, 59
Great Terror 34, 47
gulag 20, 35, 36, 39, 45

H I J K

headgear/headdresses 12–14, 20, 49, 50, 52; *kokoshnik* 12, 51; *shapka* 52
horsemanship 9, 21–23, 26, 33
hunting 11, 13, 25
hydroelectric power 14, 15
hydrogen bomb 40, 41
iconostasis 18
icons 18, 46, 47, 50; restoration of 47
imperial expansion 22, 23
industrialization/factories 34, 35, 37–39
Ivan III 9
Ivan IV (the Terrible) 9, 20, 23, 26
izba 16
jewellery 8, 15, 20
Kalmyk 12
Kandinsky, Vasili 46
Kapitza, Pyotr 41
Kazakhstan 12, 23
Kazan 20, 23
Kennedy, John F. 37
Khmelnitsky, Bogdan 22
Khrushchev, Nikita 36, 37
Kievan Rus 8
Kiev 8
Komsomol 39, 53
Korolev/Glushkov 41
Kremlin 25–27, 30, 45, 58, 59
Kutuzov, Mikhail 22

L M N

Lake Baikal 10, 39
lapti 17, 33
Lenin, Vladimir 26, 29–32, 34, 35, 57
Lermontov, Mikhail 44
literacy 42, 43
Lomonosov, Mikhail 40
Louis XIV (of France) 24
lubok 42, 51
Mahmet, Ediger 20
Mandelshtam, Osip 44, 45
Marconi, Guglielmo 40

Marshak, Samuel 53
Marx, Karl 32
May Day 34, 56, 57
Mendeleyev, Dmitry 41
Mensheviks 31
military parades 56, 57
mining 14, 39
mir (commune) 17
Moldova/Moldavia 23, 59
monasteries 18
Mongols/Golden Horde 8, 9, 12, 13
Morozov, Pavlik 53
Moscow 8, 12, 14, 16, 20, 22, 24–26, 30, 34, 36, 37, 39, 43, 46, 48, 51, 55, 59; metro 37; University 36, 40
Motherhood Medal 35
Mukhina, Vera 37
Muscovy 8, 9
music 48, 49;
Nakhimov, Admiral 55
needlecraft 12, 17, 50–53
New Economic Policy 32
Nganasan 13
Nicholas I 20, 25
Nicholas II 20, 21, 24, 25, 30–32
Nijinsky, Vaslav 48, 49
Nikon, Patriarch 18
nomads/herders 13, 23
Nobel Prize 40, 41, 45
Nureyev, Rudolf 48

O P R

October Revolution 17, 18, 20, 24, 26, 28–32, 35–38, 43, 54, 56
Octobrists 53
Old Believers 18
Old Church Slavonic 19
Oleg, Prince 8
Olga, Princess 24
onion domes 26, 27, 29, 57; construction of 27
Order of the Red Banner 33
Orlov, Count Grigory 25
Orthodox Church 9, 18–19, 45, 49, 51, 56, 57; Christmas 56; Easter 56; white/black clergy 18, 19
Palace of the Soviets 34
Pasternak, Boris 44, 45
Paul, Emperor 25
Pavlov, Ivan 40
Pavlova, Anna 48
peasants/serfs 16, 17, 20, 30, 35, 49–53; liberation 16, 17;
perestroika 36, 58
permafrost 11, 15, 39
Peter I (the Great) 16, 18, 20–22, 25, 26, 28, 29
Peter III 16
Peter/Paul Fortress 20, 28

Peterhof Palace 29
Petipa, Marius 48
politburo 31
Popov, Alexander 40
postal system 42
pottery/metalwork 44, 50, 51, 55
Pravda 43
Prokofiev, Sergei 48
Provisional Government 30, 32
Pushkin, Alexander 18, 44
railways 14, 33, 34, 38, 39, 42; BAM 39; passengers 39; Trans-Siberian 39
Rasputin, Grigori 30
Rastrelli, Bartolomeo 28, 29
Red Army 32, 33, 36
Red Guards 31, 33
Red Square 26, 27, 34, 57, 58
Repin, Ilya 46, 47
Resurrection Gate 58
rocks/minerals 14–15, 19, 24, 25, 28, 29, 38; amber 14, 29; diamond 14, 24; gold 14, 19, 24, 25, 28, 29; malachite 15; ruby 24
Roerich, Nikolai 49
Romanov, Mikhail 20
Romanovs 20, 21, 25
rouble 58
Rublev, Andrei 46, 47
Rurik, Prince of Novgorod 8
Russian Federation 58, 59
Ryazan 12
Rurikids 20

S T U

Saints: Andrew 9; Cyril 19, 42; George 9, 21, 46; Methodius 19, 42; Nicholas 27; Sergius 18
Sakharov, Andrei 40
Samoyed-Nenets 13
samovar/tea-drinking 55
sarafan 12, 17, 52
science/technology 40–43
sculpture/painting 29, 35–37, 45–47, 57
secret police: *Cheka* 36; KGB/NKVD 20, 34, 36; Okhrana 20
Shostakovich, Dmitri 48
Siberia 8–16, 20, 22, 23, 31, 32, 38, 39, 44, 45
Slavs, eastern 8
Solzhenitsyn, A. 44, 45
Sophia, Princess 18, 20
Soviet Writers' Union 45
space exploration 40, 41; *Sputnik I* 41; *Vostok I* 41
spinning 50; *prialki* 50
sports/pastimes 54, 55;
St. Basil's Cathedral 26–28

St. Petersburg 14, 20, 22–26, 28–30, 34, 36, 39, 43, 44, 48, 55; palaces 28, 29;
Stalin, Joseph 15, 26, 31, 34–38, 41, 43, 45, 47
Stalingrad 36
steppe/tundra 11
Stravinsky, Igor 48, 49
strikes 30
Surikov 23
symbols 9, 10, 19, 21, 24, 25, 35, 37, 58, 59; hammer & sickle 35, 37, 58; tsarist flag 58, 59; wheat sheaves 37
tachanka 33
Tarkovsky, Andrei 43
Tatars 8, 9, 12, 13, 22, 23, 26
Tchaikovsky, Pyotr 48
Terem Palace 26
theatre 45, 52; children's 52
Time of Troubles 20
Tobolsk 13
Tolstoy, Leo 16, 44, 45
toys 15, 51, 52; dolls 52
traditional dress 12–14, 17, 19–21, 23, 49, 51, 52, 55
transport 10, 14, 24, 25, 33, 34, 38, 39, 42
troika 10, 11
Trotsky, Leon 31, 33–35
tsars 9, 16–18, 20–23, 28, 30, 31, 52
Tsiolkovsky, Konstantin 40
Tungus 12, 13
Ukraine 12, 22, 23, 30, 33, 44, 59
Ulanova 48
Urals 10, 13, 15, 16, 39, 59

V W Y Z

valkenki 17
Veliky, Ivan 26
Vikings/*Varangians* 8
Vladimir I 8, 18
Vladimir Monomakh 8
Vrubel 46
wars: Civil 31–33, 38, 45; Cold 36, 37; Crimean 23, 55; Northern 22; WWI 30, 39, 48; WWII 29, 34, 36, 37, 39, 45
weapons/armour 9, 22, 23, 25, 32, 33, 39
White Army 32
Winter Palace 15, 25, 28, 30
wood carving 15, 50
wood working 10, 11, 16, 18, 21–27, 33, 50
Yaroslav the Wise 8
Yeltsin, Boris 58, 59
Yermak 23
Young Pioneers 53
Zhukovsky, Nikolai 40

Acknowledgements

Dorling Kindersley would like to thank:
Tamara Igumnova, Lyudmila Savchenko, Svetlana Zhizhina, Irina Poltusova, Tatiana Sizova, Yelena Smirnova, Yulia Gudovich, Lyudmila Dementieva, and Luiza Yefimova at the History Museum, Moscow; Pavel Rubinin of the Kapitza Museum, Moscow; Professor Roman Shatalov and Tatiana Susorova at the Polytechnic Museum, Moscow; Alexander Nikonov at the Museum of Armed Forces, Moscow; Tamara Shumnaya and Irina Orlova at the Museum of the Revolution, Moscow; Alexander Chepurnoi; Sergei Romaniuk; Yevgenia Grishina; Kate Cook; Zoya Yevgenyevna of Red Square Publications; Ella Piatigorsky; Joyce Roberson and Steven Platt of the Russian Orthodox Church; David Buckton at the British Museum; Cornelissen & Son, London; Paul Cornish, Andy Hutcheson, and David Fearon at the Imperial War

Museum; The Britain-Russia Centre, London; The Earl of Pembroke and Trustees of the Wilton House Trust and photographers Ian Jackson and Andy Brown.
Consultant: Geoffrey Murrell
Researcher: Robert Graham
Illustrator: John Woodcock
Modelmaker: Peter Griffiths
Index: Marion Dent
Jacket: Chris Branfield
Design and editorial assistance: Susila Baybars, Goldberry Broad, Maggie Tingle, Darren Troughton, and Jake Williamson
Picture credits:
The publisher would like to thank the following for their permission to reproduce their photographs:
a=above, c=centre, b=below, l=left, r=right, t=top:
AISA, Barcelona: 22t, 23cb, 44c, 44b, 48bl;
Bridgeman Art Library: The Fine Art Society,

London 48 cr, Hermitage, St. Petersburg: Portrait Peter I (1723) Grigory Semyonovich 20bla, Portrait Catherine I (1729–96) Feodor Rokotov 20b, Kremlin Museums, Moscow 20cla, Lords Gallery, London 39c, Bibliotheque de L'Opera, Paris 48tl, Musee d'Orsay, Paris: Coronation of Nicholas II (1852–1929) Henri Gervex 24cl, Petit Palais, Geneva: Russian Peasants (1869–1940) Andreevich Malyavin 49cr, Private Collection 34–35b, State Russian Museum, St. Petersburg: Portrait of Rastrelli (1700–71) Pietro Rotari 28tr, Stapleton Collection 28ca, Tretyakov Gallery, Moscow: Tsar Ivan IV (1530–84) Vitor Mikhailovich 20cr, Religious Procession (1880–83) Ilya Efimovich Repin 47cbr; **e.t. archive:** 20c, 48cl; **Mary Evans Picture Library:** 9tr, 12bl, 16t, 17tl, 17bl, 19tl, 21br, 33br, 39tl, 45l, 48br; **Hulton Getty:** 8tl, 8b, 37t, 57; **Giraudon:** 23c, Lauros 19tr, 21cra; **The Ronald Grant Archive:** 43br, 45tr, 45b; **Robert Harding:** Paul van Riel 39cb; **Natural History Picture Agency:** Mirko Stelzner 11trb; **Michael Holford:** 14br; **The Hutchison Library:** 52cl,

55t, © Andzey 56t, 56br; **The Interior Archive:** 29tl; **Michael Jenner:** 28cl, 29cl, 36r, 37l; **David King Collection:** 14cl,15cbr,16cl, 20tl, 21tr, 30cl, 30bl, 30br, 31tl, 32cl, 33tl, 34cl, 34cl, 35tl, 35cl, 35bl, 36t, 38tl, 38c, 42b, 43tl, 43tr, 46t, 47bl, 52tl, 53tl, 57tr, 58br; **Frank Lane Picture Agency:** 10tr; **Mander & Mitchenson:** 49tr, 49tl; **John Massey Stewart:** 28c, 29cl; **Novosti Photo Library:** 15tr, 18cl, 23cl, 26–27cb, 30cb, 30-31b, 40cla, 40clb, 41cr, 41, 46br, 50c, 53c; **Planet Earth Pictures:** William P. Paton 11b; **Nikolai Rakhmanonov:** 14t, 18tl, 21c, 24tl, 25tr, 25c; **Rex Features:** Sipa Press 58bl, 58b; **Ellen Rooney:** 18bl, 28-29b, 29tl, 29ca; **Oxford Scientific Films:** Martyn Colbeck 11cr, Mark Hamblin 11bra, Zig Leszczynski 10cl, Owen Newman 11trb; **Topham Picturepoint:** 24b; **Trip:** M. Jenkin 27tr, B. Turner 26-27ca, N&J Wiseman 37br; **Victoria & Albert Museum:** 49tl, 49l. Jacket: all DK special photography except **The Bridgeman Art Library:** back tr; **Giraudon:** front c; **Novosti Photo Library:** back bl; **Ellen Rooney:** front r; **Trip:** back br.